The
Restoration

Joan Thirsk

READER IN ECONOMIC HISTORY
UNIVERSITY OF OXFORD

LONGMAN

PROBLEMS AND PERSPECTIVES IN HISTORY

EDITOR: H.F. KEARNEY M.A. PH.D.

A full list of titles in this series
will be found on the back cover of this book

LONGMAN GROUP LIMITED
London

*Associated companies, branches and representatives
throughout the world*

©Longman Group Ltd 1976

First published 1976
Second impression 1980

ISBN 0 582 35160 X

Printed in Hong Kong by
Wah Cheong Printing Press Co Ltd

EDITOR'S FOREWORD

'Study problems in preference to periods' was the excellent advice given by Lord Acton in his inaugural lecture at Cambridge. To accept it is one thing, to put it into practice is another. In fact, in both schools and universities the teaching of history, in depth, is often hindered by certain difficulties of a technical nature, chiefly to do with the availability of sources. In this respect, history tends to be badly off in comparison with literature or the sciences. The historical equivalents of set texts, readings or experiments, in which the student is encouraged to use his own mind, are the so-called 'special periods'. If these are to be fruitful, the student must be encouraged to deal in his own way with the problems raised by historical documents and the historiography of the issues in question and he must be made aware of the wider perspectives of history. Thus, if the enclosure movement of the sixteenth century is studied, the student might examine the historiographical explanations stretching from More's *Utopia* and Cobbett to Beresford's *Lost Villages of England*. At the same time he might also be dealing with selected documents raising important problems. Finally he might be encouraged to realize the problems of peasantries at other periods of time, including Russia and China in the nineteenth and twentieth centuries. In this particular instance, thanks to Tawney and Power, *Tudor Economic Documents,* the history teacher is comparatively well off. For other special periods the situation is much more difficult. If, however, the study of history is to encourage the development of the critical faculties as well as the memory, this approach offers the best hope. The object of this series is to go some way towards meeting these difficulties.

The general plan of volumes in the series will vary. Some historical problems lend themselves easily to a threefold division of historiography, documents and consideration of wider issues, but others do not. There has been no attempt to stretch authors upon the editorial rack and it will be noted that some volumes contain no documents. They will compensate for this by additional historiographical material.

A broad view is being taken of the limits of history. Political history will not be excluded, but a good deal of emphasis will be placed on economic, intellectual and social history. The idea has in fact grown out of the experience of a group of historians at the University of Sussex, where the student is encouraged to investigate the frontier areas between his own and related disciplines.

H. KEARNEY

CONTENTS

Acknowledgements

We are grateful to the following for permission to reproduce copyright material:
Associated Book Publishers Ltd. for extracts from *The Wealth Of Nations* by Adam Smith, edited by Edwin Cannan, published by Methuen & Co. Ltd. and for extracts from *The Origins Of Scientific Economics* by W. Letwin, also published by Methuen & Co. Ltd; A. & C. Black Ltd. for extracts from *The Making of the Restoration Settlement* by Robert Bosher and for extracts from *Economic History of England* Vol. II; British Agricultural History Society for extracts from 'The Management of Crown Lands, 1649–1660' by Ian Gentles in *Agricultural History Review* XIX; the Clarendon Press for an extract from *The Social Ideas Of Religious Leaders 1660–1688* by Richard B. Schlatter, and for extracts from *England in the Reign Of Charles II* by David Ogg (c) 1956 Oxford University Press; the author and the Economic History Society for extracts from an article entitled 'Land Owners and The Civil War' by Professor H.J. Habakkuk in *Economic History Review*, 2nd Series, XVIII (1965); *English Historical Review* for extracts from 'The Restoration Government and the Municipal Corporation' by J.H. Sacret in *English Historical Review* No. 45 1930; the Folger Shakespeare Library for extracts by William Haller, W.K. Jordan and Caroline Robbins, in *The Restoration of the Stuarts, Blessing or Disaster?*; Longman Group Ltd. for extracts from *English Social History* by G.M. Trevelyan, extracts from *History of England* by G.M. Trevelyan and extracts from *England's Apprenticeship 1603–1743* by Charles H. Wilson; the author and Macmillan, London and Basingstoke, for an extract from *The Growth of Political Stability in England 1675–1725* by J.H. Plumb (ç) J.H. Plumb; Macmillan, London and Basingstoke, for extracts from *History of England from The Accession of James II* by Lord Macaulay (1913–1915) edited by C.H. Firth; author and Macmillan, London and Basingstoke, for an extract from *King and Commons 1660–1832* by Dr. Betty Kemp, reprinted by permission of Macmillan, London and Basingstoke, and St. Martin's Press Inc, New York; Thomas Nelson & Sons

Ltd. and W.W. Norton and Co. Inc. for extracts from *Century of Revolution* by Christopher Hill (c) 1961 Christopher Hill; the author and *Past and Present* for extracts from 'Literacy and Education in England 1640–1900' by Lawrence Stone in *Past and Present* No. 42 and extracts from 'The Educational Revolution in England, 1540–1640' by Lawrence Stone in *Past and Present* No. 28 (c) World Copyright: The Past and Present Society, Corpus Christi College, Oxford. Penguin Books Ltd. for extracts from *Reformation to Industrial Revolution* (1967) by Christopher Hill (c) Christopher Hill 1967, 1969; Routledge & Kegan Paul Ltd. and Toronto University Press for an extract from *Crisis and Order in English Towns, 1500–1700*, edited by Peter Clark and Paul Slack; Royal Historical Society for extracts from 'The Re-Establishment of The Church of England, 1660–1663' by Anne Whiteman in *Transactions of the Royal Historical Society* 5th Series V (1955); Science and Society Inc. for an extract from 'Land in the English Revolution' by Christopher Hill in *Science and Society* XIII No. 1; the John Rylands University Library for an extract from 'The Reverend Richard Baxter's Last Treatise' by F.J. Powicke in *Bulletin* Vol. X; the Society for Promoting Christian Knowledge for extracts from *From Uniformity To Unity 1662–1962* by Anne Whiteman, edited by G.F. Nuttall and O. Chadwick; the author and the University of Chicago Press for extracts from 'The Impact of Charles II on Restoration Literature' by James Sutherland in *Restoration and Eighteenth-Century Literature*, 1963; and the University of Chicago Press for extracts from *The Restoration Land Settlement* in *Journal of Modern History* xxvi (1954) by Joan Thirsk.

INTRODUCTION

The Puritan revolution in England has attracted much interest in the last thirty years, the Restoration very little. Yet the course of events in 1660 sheds as much light as does the study of the previous eleven years on why and where the revolution failed. At the Restoration men deliberately turned their backs on the existing government and chose another political regime. And although the new policy and the new way of life and manners which the nation adopted may not have fulfilled all the hopes of those who brought back the king, it evidently represented an acceptable compromise. The Restoration settlement was thus a criticism of what had gone before. Why has it been so neglected?

In the twentieth century the restoration of kings evokes no sympathetic response, and this is part of the explanation. But the mood of 'political and spiritual reaction'[1] in which the Commonwealth was brought to an end is a not uncommon phenomenon in twentieth-century political experience. So it can justly be argued that while the Puritan revolution continues to excite interest and attention, the lessons of the Restoration cannot be overlooked. Had the architects of the Commonwealth built their edifice differently, more of the fabric might have been saved. The Restoration settlement measures the extent of their failure.

The decision to re-establish the monarchy was arrived at comparatively suddenly, when Richard Cromwell's weakness as a leader and the resurgence of the army awoke widespread alarm for the future. But hastening this 'precipitate measure'—the description given it by an eighteenth-century commentator[2]—was the uneasy feeling, rapidly gaining conviction, that no republican solution would be lasting. Every political institution was liable to be called in question and no firm foundation for a commonwealth could be laid. The sense that everything was impermanent and insecure from one year to the next was uppermost in the cynical pamphlets published in 1659. One of the more lighthearted

[1] The phrase used by James J. Hanford in *A Restoration Reader*, 1971, p.v.
[2] Millar, cited by Caroline Robbins in *The Restoration of the Stuarts, Blessing or Disaster?*, Folger Shakespeare Library, 1960, p. 38.

and sardonic of these conveyed the mood by posing the problem in a series of questions:

> Whether the proverb be true that an Englishman by his continual stirring of the fire shews that he never knows when a thing is well; whether it be not fitting to take down all our bells in churches that the English who are so much given to ring the changes may have no farther opportunity to ring the changes any more; whether it be not strange news that the English have almost all lost their way in their own country, and whether the several guides they chose to direct them have not brought them into a wood that they have now work enough to enquire one of another how to find the way out.[3]

A more positive verdict upon public opinion was that by Gilbert Burnet: people wanted the king back 'so matters might again fall into their old channel'.[4] The Restoration, in consequence, was not carried through in direct opposition to the general will. It was achieved peaceably and the majority may be assumed to have concurred, or at least acquiesced. In London, indeed, the crowds were positively enthusiastic. At the same time, however, the nation was groping its way along a new road, not knowing where it would lead. No conditions were imposed on Charles II; his Declaration of Breda gave a general indication of the temper of the new regime but nothing more. But by that very fact it fulfilled the immediate need better than any other statement of intent. Pacification and moderation were to be the keynotes; such watchwords were perhaps the most trenchant criticism that contemporaries directed at the Commonwealth and Protectorate.

When the hard business of arriving at a settlement got under way, of course, the difficulties of pacifying and devising a moderate policy that was satisfactory to all starkly emerged. At close quarters with reality, some attitudes hardened, some were changed. Contemporaries on all sides shifted their ground as the settlement unfolded. The most articulate, critical, and dissatisfied of those who lived through the experience were, not unnaturally, the Royalists. They could pronounce their views with impunity, and they continued longest to bemoan the final outcome. But the

---

[3] B.M., Thomason Tract E986 (10), *Endless Queries or an end to Queries*, 13 June 1659.
[4] *Bishop Burnet's History of His Own Time (1723)*, 1857 edn, I, p. 55.

strange psychological atmosphere in which the new pattern of national life was worked out, on which contemporaries wrote eloquently, wore itself out in the course of one generation, and men who had not been personally involved in the events of 1640–62 began to see them in fresh perspective. Since that time, viewpoints have again altered as other European revolutions have supervened, bringing their own forms of counter revolution in their wake. The Restoration settlement now presents a fascinating kaleidoscope of opinion, as the problem has been judged in changing perspective.

In this volume five facets of the Restoration are illustrated in passages drawn from the writing of contemporaries and later historians. Since the date of their writings is significant, all the passages selected here are presented in a broadly chronological order, and the date of each commentary is given prominence in the title. In this way the Restoration can be observed, first, in anticipation; then in course of negotiation; then as it was judged by contemporaries; and finally as it has been assessed by nineteenth- and twentieth-century historians. It is noteworthy that all commentators including those living most closely to the events have been able to see in all except the religious settlement a certain unity in the policies and tendencies of the time, and have attributed much influence to the personality of Charles II. It is also instructive to observe how some of the problems which loomed largest at the time have since moved out of sharp focus, while others which occupied contemporaries least have now moved to the centre of the stage. The judgment of every generation is firmly framed by its own experience and reflects the preoccupations of its time.

Since the Restoration contained many of the elements of a fresh start, its promoters faced problems at every turn. All aspects of life came under review, for the nation had to be pacified. How much of the old monarchical regime was to be restored? How many of the innovations under the Commonwealth and Protectorate were to be preserved? How could old enemies meet again on new terms? Could some enemies even be engaged as friends? Large and small questions crowded in on contemporaries all at once and demanded prompt answers.

In these circumstances the task was greatly eased by the predominantly moderate and conciliatory mood of those who had the greatest influence over political events. General Monk himself had kept his own counsel to the very last moment, and by waiting for events to play into his hands had achieved his object without bloodshed or violence. Charles II had issued a wise and placatory declaration of his intentions. Moreover, as James Macpherson phrased it in 1775, party spirit was greatly checked by fears of a renewal of violence. Thus moderation and prudence silenced the voices of the realists who might have insisted on immediate answers to awkward questions. Instead, men consented to wait and see. This muted spirit of vindictiveness was perhaps the most remarkable feature of the Restoration settlement that accounts for its stability.

Readiness to allow events to take their course, intervening only to damp down animosity and discourage the revival of bitter recriminations, represented the mood of Charles II himself and was entirely in tune with his temperament. All descriptions of his character have said much the same thing in different words: he was disarmingly gracious to all men, no matter what their station in life. He could accommodate and dissimulate with the greatest of ease, because he cared so little about the serious issues that tore other men apart. 'Of a man who was so capable of choosing, he chose as seldom as any man that ever lived', wrote George Savile, marquis of Halifax.[5] 'Adhering strictly to no principle himself', wrote James Macpherson in 1775, 'he was not much offended at the want of it in others.' He had the right temper for the job that confronted him in 1660. Inevitably he disappointed many in the outcome. But it was only in the light of after events, when men had lived through the deposition of James II, that they began to claim it a great mistake to have brought Charles back without conditions. Gilbert Burnet put this view when he wrote in Anne's reign.[6] But in 1659–60 when the future was uncertain, lively recent experience understandably led men to agree that a restoration was only possible if it was contrived speedily without conditions. This view has since prevailed. When

[5] Cited in G.M. Trevelyan, *England under the Stuarts,* 1933 edn, p. 351. The feuds he conducted were few, though they were more conspicuous as he aged. On this, see J.P. Kenyon, *The Stuarts: A study in English kingship,* 1958, chapter 4.

[6] *Burnet's History*, I, p. 59.

John Lingard,[7] the Catholic historian, writing in 1829, revived the
charge against Monk of negligence or perfidy because 'a door
had been left open to the recurrence of dissension between the
Crown and the people', and this had made a second revolution
necessary in 1688, Macaulay rounded on him with a characteristi-
cally emphatic denunciation:

> The exact partition of power among King, Lords, and Commons,
> might well be postponed till it had been decided whether
> England should be governed by King, Lords, and Commons,
> or by cuirassiers and pikemen. Had the statesmen of the Con-
> vention taken a different course, had they held long debates on
> the principles of government, had they drawn up a new con-
> stitution and sent it to Charles, had conferences been opened,
> had couriers been passing and repassing during some weeks
> between Westminster and the Netherlands, with projects and
> counterprojects, replies by Hyde and rejoinders by Prynne,
> the coalition on which the public safety depended would have
> been dissolved: the Presbyterians and Royalists would certainly
> have quarrelled: the military factions might possibly have been
> reconciled; and the misjudging friends of liberty might long
> have regretted, under a rule worse than that of the worst
> Stuart, the golden opportunity which had been suffered to
> escape.[8]

One of the first requirements of a lasting political settlement at
the Restoration was a satisfactory separation of executive, legislative, and judicial powers. This lesson had been taught by bitter
experience during the Interregnum, and both Republicans and
Royalists recognized its wisdom, the Royalists making a place for
the king by ranking him along with, but not as part of the executive.
In fact a workable system did emerge, but it evolved pragmatically
without much intervention on the part of the king. His careless
indifference to government and his willingness to leave matters
to Clarendon was probably the best practical course he could have
chosen, though he did not select it for the best reasons. Clarendon
had a foot in both camps: he was a fervent upholder of the liberties

[7] J. Lingard, *A History of England*, 1829, VII, p. 343.
[8] T.B. Macaulay, *The History of England from the Accession of James II*, ed. C.H.
Firth, 1913, I, 133–4.

of England, as well as of the rights of the Crown.[9] In the uneasy years immediately after 1660 he effectively played the role of buffer between Crown and Parliament, promoting cooperation between them and delaying a collision of their interests. Probably no one could have held this position effectively for ever, and certainly Clarendon did not. But when the collision did occur, the existence of monarchy itself was not called in question.

As for the rise of the Whig and Tory parties, we can nowadays hardly envisage any other means of political action except through organized parties, and see no reason to seek for mistakes in Charles II's reign to account for them. This is in marked contrast to the anxious reflections of Lord Ailesbury who saw in his lifetime the burning resentments of unrequited Royalists, knew their long memories, and found in these things, regretfully, the only satisfactory explanation for the emergence of party politics (see below, p. 7)

The land settlement evolved likewise and was not a rushed administrative decision imposing a tidily uniform solution. The problem only slowly revealed itself in its full dimensions, and as it did so public and Parliamentary opinion crystallized around a policy that was reasonably fair both to Royalist, Crown, and Church owners, and to Commonwealth purchasers. No settlement could have satisfied everyone, but this one had the merit of removing all possibility of concerted opposition. It satisfied a sufficient number of people in both camps: some Royalists were content with what they recovered, some were bitter at their losses; some Commonwealth purchasers were grateful for favourable leases of their purchases, some were angry to be dispossessed. The land settlement had appeared to contemporaries as one of the two chief obstacles to a restoration of the monarchy. In fact James Macpherson's judgment of the political settlement applies equally well to the land settlement: 'Everything fell sooner than could have been expected into regularity and form.'[10] The concern of recent historians to identify more precisely the lasting effects of the land sales presents the problem in a new perspective. Seen in the light of other large confiscations of land, like that which accompanied the dissolution of the monasteries, or the confiscations

---

[9] *Burnet's History*, I, p. 104.
[10] James Macpherson, *The History of Great Britain...*, 1775, I, p. 5.

of land at the French Revolution, its long-term consequences are now being assessed, first, in terms of the permanent changes of ownership, which were relatively few, and secondly, in terms of changes in land use and attitudes towards land management, which crept in during the Interregnum and survived the Restoration.

The thorniest problem of all was the religious settlement, for religious fervour took longest to cool.[11] It was the most controversial at the time and has remained so ever since. Many contemporaries thought that a generous Church settlement was intended. The king in his Declaration of Breda and in his later interventions in the Parliamentary and churchmen's debates held loyally to the one opinion in favour of toleration. Had his view prevailed, the Restoration settlement would rank high in the judgment of presentday historians as a triumph of wise diplomacy on all fronts. In fact, the Anglican clergy made the settlement in a frame of mind that hardened noticeably between 1660 and 1662, producing a 'solution' which, in the opinion of some, flagrantly violated the intentions of the Declaration of Breda.[12] This explains the lurking sense of guilt which still underlies much of the literature from the pens of churchmen justifying the policy. But a more severe criticism lies in the fact that the religious settlement turned the formerly comprehensive English Church into a persecuting one and divided the nation in two. Since the division not only defined religious persuasion, but also ran along class lines it deepened social divisions that were being more firmly emphasised elsewhere by conservative politicians and acquisitive commercial interests. Our class-conscious society in the twentieth century, which affronts so many visitors from younger continents, grew some of its deepest and strongest roots in the 1660s when those stems which had been cut short by the Puritan revolution, surged again at the Restoration with redoubled vigour. The presentday historian perhaps sees these things more clearly and regretfully than any earlier generation.

An even stronger preoccupation of twentieth-century historians, however, is the long-term consequence of the religious settlement for Nonconformists. The historical assessment of this issue has undergone a marked change since the seventeenth century.

[11] *Ibid.*, I, p. 41.
[12] This view is strongly put by John Lingard, in his *History of England,* 1829, VII, p. 424.

Contemporaries saw its effects in personal terms, in the circumscribed lives of men whom they knew personally and respected, who could so obviously have played a distinguished role in public life had they conformed. Historians, on the other hand, have gradually learned to see their disabilities in a more positive light. Nonconformists were compelled to employ their energies elsewhere, especially in industry and commerce, and because of these constraints, they invigorated economic and intellectual life. Indeed, successive generations of English historians have depicted the unexpected benefits of religious intolerance in ever brightening colours. At least one American historian, in contrast, has recently dwelt on the losses, speculating whether the presence of Dissenters in Parliament might not have averted the American Revolution.[13]

The theme that is noticeably absent so far from most discussions of the religious settlement concerns the reactions of ordinary people in town and country to the decisions taken in London. In insisting on uniformity, it is not yet clear whether the bishops and the Parliament accurately reflected the mood of the nation as a whole or of one influential section of the gentry class. Were they not also reacting excessively to Baxter's handling of the debates at the Savoy conference, and the alarms provoked by events in London such as Venner's Rising? Their deepest fear was of the Catholics, but it coloured their view of the Puritans as well. Our hindsight makes it difficult to see the situation through the eyes of contemporaries. Anglicans could not then see that Dissent would become a strong and abiding force in national life. Many thought it an aberration encouraged by dissident clergymen which would be easily cured if the clergy would teach their flock to conform (see below, p. 67). Events proved them wrong, but just how soon the nation taught its Anglican clergy that they had misjudged the mood of the people is not altogether clear. The historical debate on the religious settlement has revived in recent years, and the final word has not yet been said. But it is noticeable that recent reassessments still concentrate their main attention on official policy and pay little heed to the *modus vivendi* devised by people in their local communities. In every village and town ordinary men and women interpreted and adapted national policy according to their own lights, just as many of them had

---

[13] Robbins, *The Restoration of the Stuarts*, p. 41.

fought the Civil War on their own local terms, setting local loyalties alongside, if not above, their loyalty to the nation. These same people passed their own verdict on the religious settlement, but that history has yet to be written.

An aspect of the Restoration which has received the most thoughtful consideration only in the twentieth century is its economic consequences. To set the scene for the debate on this issue it is necessary to re-read some of the leading economic writers of the later seventeenth century.

G.B. Hertz in a sensitive analysis of this pamphlet literature, carried out in 1902, saw the Restoration as 'the seed time of the Empire'.

> Public opinion under Charles II was coloured throughout by a mercantile ambition which foreshadowed the later evolution of the national character, and differentiated the age from the previous times when dynastic and theological considerations ruled every act of state. In 1688 the typical Englishman looked on maritime and commercial enterprise as the ideal mission of his race. . . . Trade had taken the place of religion as the pivot of international relations, and even the most Christian king ascribed success not to the better faith but to the last pistole.[14]

Hertz was writing when the Empire was uncritically assumed to be a proud, positive achievement which was secure for all time.

Since then a clearer view of the sixteenth-century phase of aggressive expansionism into new continents has given Hertz's verdict an old-fashioned look, though it would still be possible to argue that a *qualitative* change in the fervour of imperialist ambitions occurred at the Restoration. But instead the discussion of economic development and policy is now concerned rather with their continuity or discontinuity during the Interregnum and Charles II's reign. Obvious continuities are several: some of the same economic advisers continued to command authority through both periods; the economic debates which were resumed in 1660 had an old familiar ring, sharpened only by additional experience; Charles II's government developed further the use of committees to shape policy just as they had been used under the Commonwealth and Protectorate, and as Charles I and his predecessors had used

[14] G.B. Hertz, *English Public Opinion after the Restoration*, T. Fisher Unwin, London, 1902.

them earlier still in exceptional moments of economic difficulty. But is it nevertheless possible to see beyond these superficial signs of continuity a decisive break in policy and a fundamental change in economic assumptions somewhere between 1640 and 1670?

William Cunningham, spanning the turn of the nineteenth and twentieth centuries, ventured one of the first judgments on this score. He deemed the Interregnum a period of quiescence or stagnation that was followed by a wave of energetic economic expansion as the threads of activity, dropped in 1642, were resumed.[15] But Cunningham had not done all the spadework which twentieth-century historians consider necessary before enunciating his views of the age, and Lipson's new analysis in 1931 was more challenging and exciting in positing an economic divide at the Interregnum between the regulated economy of the past and the *laissez-faire* of the future. In this interpretation Lipson has been followed by Christopher Hill, who maintains that a vigorous new economic policy was inaugurated by the revolution and a new business ethos dictated by the bourgeoisie at the Restoration. Charles Wilson argues differently: he sees a continuous ebb and flow in debates and decisions throughout the seventeenth century and cannot discern a new unity among middle-class business men at the Restoration, consistently pursuing their interests at the expense of the labouring classes.

While disagreement continues, then, on whether the Interregnum and Restoration mark significant watersheds in economic development, no one denies that in the long term a shift can be discerned between 1600 and 1700 in the weight of opinion supporting a policy of *laissez-faire* and turning away from the idea of the regulated economy. It is visible in the measures taken by 1700 to withdraw the privileges of the monopoly trading companies which the Crown had so strongly defended in 1600. It is visible also in the arguments of economic writers who were the first to see that events were silently stealing a march on the policy makers. Many new industries in the seventeenth century quietly expanded in the dark interstices of the regulated economy, and found their markets without fuss or commotion in small towns and villages within the kingdom. Economic writers began to glimpse the truth, when, instead of devoting their interminable debates to overseas trade,

[15] W. Cunningham, *The Growth of English Industry and Commerce in Modern Times*, 1919, II, 1, pp. 193-4. This work was first published in one volume in 1882.

they began to discuss the opportunities that lay in the freer home market: they campaigned for improved transport facilities; they joined in a controversy about the increasing competition between itinerant pedlars and urban shopkeepers; they saw the role of labour in industrial production in fresh terms. The stage was being set for Adam Smith in the eighteenth century to become the eloquent theorist on the newly perceived realities of economic life.

Economic experience after 1660 gradually paved the way for a more efficient organization of working-class labour that would make the poor work more and loiter less. Meanwhile different standards were being enjoined upon the upper classes. Political conservatism at the Restoration restored the gentry to their old seats of local power, and they sank into them with relief and satisfaction, determined not to stir again. Some dedicated themselves to rehabilitating their fortunes, some to rehabilitating the authority of their class in local society. The psychological shocks and injuries of the Interregnum lived with them for the rest of their lives and saddled them with prejudices which historians necessarily see as ephemeral influences. But in many varied fields of social life, in the subsequent history of education, in the legal devices used by the gentry to protect their estates, in attitudes towards the poor, we see the lingering consequences: barriers were being erected against social mobility which bore the hallmarks of counterrevolution.

Macaulay, not surprisingly in the context of his time, had no clear perception of the hardening class structure as it evolved at the Restoration. It was still firmly built into his own upbringing and environment, and he did not challenge it. In the twentieth century it appears as a more precarious edifice. Its framework is examined in general descriptive terms by Trevelyan in his *Social History* and in more rigorous analytical terms in such studies as those of H. J. Habakkuk and others on the composition of the landed gentry class. At present the picture is still only partial: the shape of the urban middle class, of the professional, and of the labouring classes is still sketched in shadowy outline. But the twentieth-century historian has at least begun to paint with a finer brush the lineaments of *all* the social classes as they reformed their ranks after the revolution.

The 'almost instantaneous revolution' which occurred in manners and morals at the Restoration was one of the great surprises to contemporaries, prompting stern censure from the older generation, and continuing to shock nineteenth-century historians in equal measure. Macaulay's condemnation was delivered in stentorian tones. A ready explanation was found at the time, and has been often repeated since, that it was a reaction against Puritanism, and was further encouraged by Charles II's own personality and preferences. 'The ruin of his reign and of all his affairs,' wrote Burnet, 'was occasioned chiefly by his delivering himself up at his first coming over to a mad range of pleasure.'[16] The task of explanation may well prove harder for future historians. As fashions and moral standards move towards a more relaxed discipline in the 1960s and 1970s, some marked similarities with Charles II's reign have been noted. We have yet to see into what fresh channel this stream of influences will next be diverted. In the seventeenth century the licentious tone of Restoration literature gave way to another style of writing. Through the medium of satire, writers like Dryden and Swift fought the next battle on the side of virtue, to inaugurate the Age of Reason. We lack perspective on our own time, but the historian who will one day judge our age may well feel that the current explanation for the revolution in manners and morals that occurred at the Restoration is incomplete, and viewing it in the longer perspective afforded by twentieth-century experience, will offer a more perceptive and less simple commentary.

[16] *Burnet's History*, I, p. 61.

THE DECLARATION OF BREDA

Since Charles II returned to England 'without any other conditions than what had been frankly offered by himself in his Declaration and Letters from Breda'* the Declaration was the document to which constant reference was made in the next two years. It therefore takes precedence here over all commentaries on the Restoration.

CHARLES R.

Charles, by the grace of God, king of England, Scotland, France and Ireland, Defender of the Faith, &c., to all our loving subjects, of what degree or quality soever, greeting.

If the general distraction and confusion which is spread over the whole kingdom doth not awaken all men to a desire and longing that those wounds which have so many years together been kept bleeding may be bound up, all we can say will be to no purpose. However, after this long silence we have thought it our duty to declare how much we desire to contribute thereunto, and that as we can never give over the hope in good time to obtain the possession of that right which God and nature hath made our due, so we do make it our daily suit to the Divine Providence that he will, in compassion to us and our subjects after so long misery and sufferings, remit and put us into a quiet and peaceable possession of that our right, with as little blood and damage to our people as is possible. Nor do we desire more to enjoy what is ours than that all our subjects may enjoy what by law is theirs, by a full and entire administration of justice throughout the land, and by extending our mercy where it is wanted and deserved.

And to the end that the fear of punishment may not engage any, conscious to themselves of what is past, to a perseverance in guilt for the future, by opposing the quiet and happiness of their country in the restoration both of king, peers and people to their just, ancient and fundamental rights, we do by these presents declare that we do grant a free and general pardon, which we are ready upon demand to pass under our great seal of England, to all our subjects, of what degree or quality soever, who

*Clarendon's words in his autobiography, 3rd edn, 1761, II, p. 1.

within forty days after the publishing hereof shall lay hold upon this our grace and favour, and shall by any public act declare their doing so, and that they return to the loyalty and obedience of good subjects (excepting only such persons as shall hereafter be excepted by Parliament). Those only excepted, let all our loving subjects, how faulty soever, rely upon the word of a king, solemnly given by this present declaration, that no crime whatsoever committed against us or our royal father before the publication of this shall ever rise in judgment or be brought in question against any of them, to the least endamagement of them, either in their lives, liberties or estates, or (as far forth as lies in our power) so much as to the prejudice of their reputations by any reproach or term of distinction from the rest of our best subjects; we desiring and ordaining that henceforward all notes of discord, separation and difference of parties be utterly abolished among all our subjects, whom we invite and conjure to a perfect union among themselves, under our protection, for the re-settlement of our just rights and theirs in a free Parliament, by which, upon the word of a king, we will be advised.

And because the passion and uncharitableness of the times have produced several opinions in religion, by which men are engaged in parties and animosities against each other, which, when they shall hereafter unite in a freedom of conversation, will be composed or better understood, we do declare a liberty to tender consciences, and that no man shall be disquieted or called in question for differences of opinion in matter of religion which do not disturb the peace of the kingdom; and that we shall be ready to consent to such an Act of Parliament as upon mature deliberation shall be offered to us for the full granting that indulgence.

And because, in the continued distractions of so many years and so many and great revolutions, many grants and purchases of estates have been made to and by many officers, soldiers and others, who are now possessed of the same and who may be liable to actions at law upon several titles, we are likewise willing that all such differences, and all things relating to such grants, sales and purchases, shall be determined in Parliament, which can best provide for the just satisfaction of all men who are concerned.

And we do further declare that we will be ready to consent to any Act or Acts of Parliament to the purposes aforesaid, and for the full satisfaction of all arrears due to the officers and soldiers of the army under the command of General Monck, and that they shall be received into our service upon as good pay and conditions as they now enjoy.

Given under our sign manual and privy signet,
at our court at Breda,
this 4/14 day of April 1660,
in the twelfth year of our reign.

Lords Journals, XI, pp. 7–8.

Part One

THE POLITICAL SETTLEMENT

The political settlement posed a short-term and a long-term problem simultaneously. How was Charles to reward his followers for their loyalty and yet reduce antagonisms between them and his newfound friends among the Parliamentarians so that government could get under way again? The long-term problem raised still more difficult issues: how was the power of central government to be divided between king, executive, and Parliament? Which classes in the nation were to be trusted to govern locally?

The advice offered by the Royalist Duke of Newcastle to Charles II expressed frank self-interest on the subject of rewarding the king's friends (1, i)*. On the best way to achieve a *modus vivendi* between Crown and Parliament his advice was limited, though, as far as it went, realistic (1, ii): the king must secure adequate financial provision and so ensure to himself some measure of independence. His advice on foreign policy expressed an utterly cynical view of politics and the people, not uncommon among Royalists who lacked all sympathy and understanding for the Good Old Cause, but worth recalling in the light of the foreign policy actually pursued (1, iii).

The Act of Indemnity and Oblivion was the first and most significant act of statesmanship towards achieving a settlement. It had to be virtually all-embracing or it would have led to endless bickerings (2). Indeed, whatever solution was adopted, it could not overnight eradicate tensions between people in their everyday lives (3). As it worked out, it left a legacy of much bitterness among the Royalist party (4), and in the view of Lord Ailesbury, sowed the seeds of Whiggism (5). Nowadays, on the other hand, its profound good sense is acknowledged (6).

Many Presbyterians and former Parliament men exerted influence

*Numbers in brackets refer to the extracts which follow.

in the restored Parliament (7, 8) while the Royalists tended to quarrel with the Court and with each other. According to Clarendon (9) Royalists failed in government because they had been corrupted by the unsettled life they had led for nearly two decades, and were incapable of discharging the responsible duties of administration with honesty and seriousness. Macaulay wrote eloquently on the same lines (10). Presentday historians pay little heed to the psychological atmosphere created by a counter-revolution, and direct their attention to the actions of the men who did govern and the long-term consequences.

David Ogg describes the development of the practical machinery of government, as it evolved pragmatically under Charles II. The Privy Council had the same manifold concerns as the Privy Council under Charles I, but it learned from the experience of the Commonwealth and Protectorate to delegate work to committees. Secretaries of the Privy Council became increasingly important agents of communication between executive and legislature (11). Betty Kemp describes how Parliament resumed the quest for a balance of power between King and Commons, though the Restoration marks merely one stage along the road (12). Experience during the Interregnum when Parliament held the sovereign power had drawn attention to the special dangers of committing legislative and executive powers to the same body. Pragmatically rather than deliberately, a solution was arrived at which contrived a system of checks and balances (13).

At the centre and in the localities, effective power was restored to the landed classes (14, 15). This was exactly what the Royalist Duke of Newcastle had advocated when he offered advice on granting privileges to corporate towns (17). In their own parishes the Anglican gentry were so influential that they could, and when it suited their interests they did, reduce all law and central government to naught (16). But they were not considered by the Crown as a serious threat to monarchical interests. In the towns, on the other hand, where the Crown felt less sure of the support of its local administrators, and where republican sympathies were still nurtured, Charles made a crude and thoroughly misguided attempt to establish direct control over their governing bodies (18). He thus stirred up simmering discontent that was perhaps more serious than the seditious ideas he had intended to root out by his attack on the corporations.

Royalist Advice at the Restoration

1 The Duke of Newcastle, 1660

i. *How to reward friends*

Now, Sir, with your Majesty's favour, I will speak of the greatest error of state that ever was committed in these two last reigns and that is, they ever rewarded their enemies, and neglected their friends. That this is an undeniable truth so public to the view of all the world, as some divines have been raised for it, though few, but abundance of lawyers, noblemen and gentlemen, this way to make them noblemen. This was but a weak policy to take off enemies. Nay, they would say: he was a shrewd man, we must please him, reward him, make him a lord, give him office. But for a friend, he is an honest man, give him nothing, he'll do us no hurt. Certainly, this policy was brought out of the Indies, where they pray to the Devil and not to God, for they say God's a good man, and will do nobody hurt. Therefore, they will pray and flatter the Devil that may hurt them. What man almost hath been raised these two reigns that did not oppose the king and the state? Nay, they had no other way to raise themselves, they thought, and therefore they plied it, which was the ruin of our kingdom. . . . This made Parliament so refractory to his Majesty, everyone opposing, thinking to be raised. . . . To make enemies and destroy friends—a most pernicious maxim and a false one as ever was in the world.

ii. *How to control Parliament through the purse*

The greatest error in these last two reigns were that the kings always wanted money, which is the greatest error. . . . When you are rich and call a Parliament, your Majesty is then master of the

3

field and you may do what you please, and then they have no ground to work of against you. Oh, riches, Sir, in a king is more advantageous both at home and abroad than I can express. Therefore, Sir, put your money in your purse and be rich. There is nothing better than to govern by well-regulated Parliaments. And if your Majesty be not necessitated but rich, they will be regular. Parliaments should be kept within their bounds which everybody knows.

iii. *How to achieve domestic peace by foreign wars*

The advantages of a foreign war and with these two kings in their turns [i.e. the kings of France and Spain] are first, they will be so weakened as your Majesty needs not fear them for any invasion. Then it will enrich your Majesty's kingdom very much; increase your Majesty's shipping; busy your people, and the looser sort, as also the better sort, to be full of employments; vent the overplus that would be a burthen to the kingdom; make your people warlike and especially by sea, which is your Majesty's greatest strength, for making a foreign war keeps your Majesty safe at home both from invasion and a civil war, when a soft and long peace makes a civil war, fomented by divines and lawyers, for the people must be busied with something or else they will find work themselves, though to the ruin of the kingdom. Therefore, there is nothing like a foreign war for your Majesty's safety and honour, for the good of your people and kingdoms.

Clarendon MS 109, ff. 60–61, 57–8, 87–8, Bodleian Library, Oxford.

The Act of Indemnity and Oblivion

2 Edward Hyde, later Lord Clarendon, 1660

Speech in the House of Commons, September, 1660

His Majesty well knows that, by this Act, he hath gratified and obliged many worthy and pious men who have contributed much to his Restoration...but he is not sure that he may not likewise have gratified some who did neither contribute to his coming in, nor are yet glad that he is in.

From William Cobbett, *The Parliamentary History of England,* 1808, IV, 128.

3 Lord Clarendon: later reflections, 1672

Men were well enough contented that the king should grant indemnity to all men that had rebelled against him, that he should grant their lives and fortunes to them who had forfeited them to him. But they thought it very unreasonable and unjust that the king should release those debts which were immediately due to them, and forgive those trespasses which had been committed to their particular damage. They could not endure to meet the same men in the king's highway, now it was the king's highway again, who had heretofore affronted them in those ways because they were not the king's and only because they knew they could obtain no justice against them. They could not with any patience see those men who not only during the war had oppressed them, plundered their houses, and had their own adorned with the furniture they had robbed them of, ride upon the same horses which they had then taken from them upon no other pretence but because they were better than their own. But after the war was ended, had committed many insolent trespasses upon them wantonly, and to shew their power of justice of peace or committee men, and had from the lowest beggary raised great estates out of which they were well able to satisfy, at least in some degree, the damages the other had sustained. And those and other passions of this kind, which must have invalidated the whole Act of Indemnity, could not have been extinguished without the king's influence, and indeed his immediate interposition and industry.

The Life of Edward Earl of Clarendon, written by Himself, 3rd edn, Oxford, 1761, 11, 180–1.

4   Bishop Burnet, *c.* 1700

The act of indemnity passed with very few exceptions, at which the cavaliers were highly dissatisfied, and made great complaints of it. In the disposal of offices and places, as it was not possible to gratify all, so there was little regard had to men's merits or services. When the cavaliers saw they had not that share in places that they expected, they complained of it so highly, that the Earl of Clarendon, to excuse the king's passing them by, was apt to beat down the value they set on their services. This laid the foundation of an implacable hatred in many of them, that was completed by the extent and comprehensiveness of the Act of Indemnity, which cut off their hopes of being reimbursed out of the fines, if not the confiscations of those who had during the course of the wars been on the parliament's side. It is true, the first Parliament, called, by way of derogation, the Convention, had been too much on that side not to secure themselves and their friends: so they took care to have the most comprehensive words put in it that could be thought of. But when the new Parliament was called a year after, in which there was a design to set aside the Act of Indemnity, and to have brought in a new one, the king did so positively insist on his adhering to the Act of Indemnity, that the design of breaking into it was laid aside. The Earl of Clarendon owned it was his counsel. Acts or promises of indemnity, he thought, ought to be held sacred: a fidelity in the observation of them was the only foundation, upon which any government could hope to quiet seditions, or civil wars: and if people once thought, that those promises were only made to deceive them, without an intention to observe them religiously, they would never for the future hearken to any treaty. He often said, 'it was the making those promises had brought the king home, and it was the keeping them must keep him at home.' So that whole work from beginning to the end was entirely his. The angry men, that were thus disappointed of all their hopes, made a jest of the title of it, 'An act of oblivion and of indemnity'; and said, 'the king had passed an act of oblivion for his friends, and of indemnity for his enemies.' To load the earl of Clarendon the more, it was given out that he advised the king to gain his enemies, since he was sure of his friends by their principles. With this he was often charged, though he always denied it. Whether the king fastened it upon him after he had disgraced him, to make him the more odious, I cannot tell.

Gilbert Burnet, 1643–1715, Whig Bishop of Salisbury from 1689: his *History of My Own Times* was published posthumously but was written circa 1700. See also p. 42 below.

5   Thomas, Earl of Ailesbury, *c.* 1728

My design by this [description of the fortunes of the Earl and Countess of Derby at the Restoration] is to set out in a true light the source of what was termed in years following 'Whiggism', and it really sprung by degrees from the discontent of noble families and of many good families of the first gentry in the counties whose ancestors were sequestered, decimated, and what not on account of their steadfast loyalties, and so many losing their lives also. I have been told that the brave Lord Biron and five sons lost their lives in several actions. The estate almost wasted, and I never heard that the heir was ever countenanced; and there were hundreds more that had the same fate amongst the nobility and gentry, many of whose children were obliged to take service in noblemen's houses. The noble historian [Clarendon] could never give the Earl of Derby scarce one good word in his history, and crowned his dislike at the Restoration towards my lord, his son, and my lady, his mother, in advising my good king and master to give the negative to that just bill [restoring the Earl of Derby to his lands], and so unpopular an action in that happy and joyful conjuncture, and for why? To favour Sergeants Maynard and Glyn, etc., who came to that lord's part of [*sic*] estate so unjustly and inhumanly. This is but one particular case, but his maxim in general was, and such he gave as advice, that His Majesty must reward his enemies to sweeten them, for that his friends were so by a settled principle, and that their loyalty could not be shaken.

Memoirs of Thomas, Earl of Ailesbury, written by Himself, Roxburghe Club, 1890, 1, 6–7.

6 J.P. Kenyon, 1966

Charles fulfilled in a handsome manner his promise of a full indemnity and oblivion. The Act of Indemnity and Oblivion is a remarkable document; with the exception of those who had signed Charles I's death warrant or officiated at his execution, plus a few particularly obnoxious individuals, like Vane, Lambert and Haslerigg, everyone received a full pardon, and all process of revenge or retribution was halted. More remarkable still, for three years penalties were imposed for reflecting, by speech or writing, on any man's conduct during the past twenty years.

The Stuart Constitution, 1603–88: documents and commentary, Cambridge University Press, 1966, p. 362.

Parties and Personalities in Government

7 Sir John Bramston, *c.* 1683

In this Convention, for I know not how it can be called a Parliament, being summoned by writs in the name of the Keepers of the Liberties, and without the Lords—but yet the King thought fit to give it the epithet of, and termed it, the Healing Parliament, and continued it after his return, until matters were settled...I say, in that Convention the old Parliament men, Hollis, Pierrepoint, Annesley, Swinfin, and others of that gang, were too crafty for us...Ere we got into the House, after the sermons in St Margaret's church were ended, they were seated (as they had contrived), and Mr Pierrepoint had named Sir Harbottle Grimston for Speaker, and they were conducting him to the chair before many others were come into the House.

And they were too crafty for that King, with the help of Sir Orlando Bridgeman, and Mr Geoffrey Palmer (who had been of the King's party all along the war, were here upon that place, and might have better informed the King and those about him); for they persuaded the King and Sir Edmund Hyde that the King could not come home but by the Presbyterians, who all trucked for employments and honours; whereas it was the Cavalier party, the loyal gentry, that brought him home in truth; for by their constancy to his interest, often plotting and contriving his restitution, though with the loss of their fortunes and hazard of their lives, together with the quarrels and differences amongst the great officers of the armies, and the general unsatisfaction of the people, tired with the oppressions and change of their governors, and the endless dividing into sects and factions, the whole nation was desirous of the King's return, without whom they see there would be no end of war and trouble. But though this is certainly true, yet the King, and those in power with him, especially Hyde, the Chancellor, believed the Presbyterians did the work, and accordingly that party, who had the money too (the Cavaliers being generally poor), got all the employments.

The Autobiography of Sir John Bramston, K.B., of Skreens in the Hundred of Chelmsford, ed. P. Braybrooke, Camden Society, 1845, pp. 116–17.

8   Roger Coke, 1694

The Presbyterians were scarce wet with the tail of this storm, none of them (except those in sequestered livings) being punished either in their persons or fortunes; and many of them were preferred into high places both in church and state. The poor Cavalier, or loyal suffering party, who hoped for a heaven upon earth in this king's reign, fell into a worse state than that they were in before.

A Detection of the Court and State of England, 3rd edn, 1697, p. 425.

9   Lord Clarendon, 1672

I have thought myself obliged to renew the memory of all these particulars that the several vicissitudes and stages may be known by which the jealousies, murmurs, and disaffections in the royal party amongst themselves, and against each other, had mounted to that height which the king found them at when he returned, when, in truth, very few men of active minds, and upon whom he could depend in any sudden occasion that might probably press him, can be named who had any confidence in each other. All men were full of bitter reflections upon the actions and behaviour of others, or of excuses and apologies for themselves for what they thought might be charged upon them. The woeful vice of drinking, from the uneasiness of their fortune, or the necessity of frequent meetings together, for which taverns were the most secure places, had spread itself very far in that *classis* of men, as well as upon other parts of the nation, in all counties; and had exceedingly weakened the parts and broken the understandings of many, who had formerly competent judgments, and had been in all respects fit for any trust; and had prevented the growth of parts in many young men who had good affections, but had been from their entering into the world so corrupted with that excess, and other licence of the time, that they only made much noise, and, by their extravagant and scandalous debauches, brought many calumnies and disestimation upon that cause which they pretended to advance.

The Life of Edward Earl of Clarendon, written by Himself, 3rd edn, Oxford, 1761, II, 34–5.

10 Lord Macaulay, 1848

Scarcely any rank or profession escaped the infection of the prevailing immorality; but those persons who made politics their business were perhaps the most corrupt part of the corrupt society. For they were exposed, not only to the same noxious influences which affected the nation generally, but also to a taint of a peculiar and of a most malignant kind. Their character had been formed amidst frequent and violent revolutions and counterrevolutions. In the course of a few years they had seen the ecclesiastical and civil polity of their country repeatedly changed. They had seen an Episcopal Church persecuting Puritans, a Puritan Church persecuting Episcopalians, and an Episcopal Church persecuting Puritans again. They had seen hereditary monarchy abolished and restored. They had seen the Long Parliament thrice supreme in the state, and thrice dissolved amidst the curses and laughter of millions. They had seen a new dynasty rapidly rising to the height of power and glory, and then on a sudden hurled down from the chair of state without a struggle. They had seen a new representative system devised, tried, and abandoned. They had seen a new House of Lords created and scattered. They had seen great masses of property violently transferred from Cavaliers to Roundheads, and from Roundheads back to Cavaliers. During these events no man could be a stirring and thriving politician who was not prepared to change with every change of fortune. It was only in retirement that any person could long keep the character either of a steady Royalist or of a steady Republican. One who, in such an age, is determined to attain civil greatness must renounce all thought of consistency. Instead of affecting immutability in the midst of endless mutation, he must be always on the watch for the indications of a coming reaction. He must seize the exact moment for deserting a falling cause. Having gone all lengths with a faction while it was uppermost, he must suddenly extricate himself from it when its difficulties begin, must assail it, must persecute it, must enter on a new career of power and prosperity in company with new associates. His situation naturally develops in him to the highest degree a peculiar class of abilities and a peculiar class of vices. He becomes quick of observation and fertile of resource. He catches without effort the tone of any sect or party with which he chances to mingle. He discerns the signs of the times with a sagacity which to the multitude appears miraculous, with a sagacity resembling that with which a veteran police officer pursues the faintest indications of crime, or with which a Mohawk warrior follows a track through the woods. But we shall seldom find in a statesman so trained, integrity, constancy, any of the virtues of the noble family of Truth. He has no faith in any doctrine, no zeal for any cause. He has seen so many old institutions swept away, that he has no reverence for prescription. He has seen so many new institutions, from which much had been expected, produce mere disappointment, that he has no hope of improvement. He sneers alike at those who are anxious to preserve and at those who are eager to reform. There is nothing in the state which he could not, without a scruple or a blush, join in defending or in destroying. Fidelity to opinions and to friends seems to him mere dullness and wrongheadedness. Politics he regards, not as a science of which the object is the happiness of mankind, but as an exciting game of mixed chance and skill, at which a dexterous and lucky player may win an estate, a coronet, perhaps a crown, and at which one rash move may lead to the loss of fortune and of life. Ambition, which, in good times, and in good minds, is half a virtue, now, disjoined from every elevated and philanthropic sentiment, becomes a selfish cupidity scarcely less ignoble than avarice. Among those politicians who, from the Restoration to the accession of the House of Hanover, were at the head of the great parties in the state, very few can be named whose reputation is not stained by what, in our age, would be called gross perfidy and corruption. It is scarcely an exaggeration to say that the most unprincipled public men who have taken part in affairs within our memory would, if tried by the standard which was in fashion during the latter part of the seventeenth century, deserve to be regarded as scrupulous and disinterested.

The History of England from the Accession of James the Second by Lord Macaulay, ed. C.H. Firth, Macmillan, 1913–15, I, 162–5.

The Executive

11   David Ogg, 1934

In the years immediately following the Restoration Charles relied on the experience and prestige of Clarendon; and in their range the chancellor's activities extended to every corner that could be reached by an active and solicitous administration, activities radiating from the privy council. Clarendon's theory of government was based on a clear-cut distinction between the spheres of executive and legislative, according to which the former was vested solely in Council, while the latter was committed to king in parliament. Over the king he exercised a tutelage which became more galling with years, and from which Charles at last emancipated himself with the help of the chancellor's enemies.

When Charles's privy council assembled for the first time in England on May 31, 1660, its composition showed a strange mixture of Royalists, Presbyterians, and old servants of the Commonwealth. In the first class were Clarendon, Southampton, Ormonde, Somerset, Lindsey, and Dorchester; in the second Northumberland, Anglesey, Say and Sele, Holles, and Robartes; in the third class were Albemarle, Sandwich, and Charles Howard, first earl of Carlisle. Its numbers steadily increased from 27 to 40 and even 50, at which point it became unwieldy....The powers of the Council were so extensive because they were undefined. It was a nebula from which the separate ministerial departments were afterwards evolved, a great clearing-house of government, presided over by a king for whose personality and ability there was still much scope....In practice many duties had to be 'committed' to specified 'committees', some of a very temporary character. In 1668 it was resolved that nothing should be decided in council until it had been considered by a committee; nor was anything to be referred to a committee until it had received preliminary consideration at the Board. In the opening years of the reign there were about thirty committees, of which two—that for naval affairs and that for plantations—were standing committees; but late in 1660, on the advice of Thomas Povey (who had served in the Commonwealth Council for the Colonies), two permanent bodies were established—a Council of Trade and a Council of Foreign Plantations. . . .

The secretariat of the privy council had acquired increased importance from both Cromwellian experience and French influence. Unless overshadowed by a great chancellor, such as Clarendon, or a great treasurer, as Danby, secretaries might, as did Arlington and Sunderland, take upon themselves many of the functions now performed by a prime minister. Primarily a household official, the secretary generally had a seat in the Commons where, on the one hand, he would be expected to facilitate the passage of measures approved by the executive; and, on the other, to face his responsibilities as an ordinary member of the House. 'As a privy councillor', said secretary Coventry in 1677, 'I have taken my oath, but as a parliament man I have my opinion.' It was not always easy to fulfil this dual function; for while, in the earlier years of the reign, the secretary was like a spring, facilitating easy communication between executive and legislature, he later became a buffer, forced to sustain the impact of a body of men increasingly conscious of their strength. . . .

Clarendon could not have foreseen that the institution which seemed to him traditional and static was destined to prove both dynamic and progressive. Nowhere else can the steady expansion of English administrative needs be seen so clearly as in the records of the privy council; in no other body could have been found the elasticity and versatility essential for handling the daily-increasing problems of an adolescent kingdom and a juvenile empire. If the principles of constitutional monarchy were not conceded in Charles's reign, at least its framework was being pieced together; and the monarch who appeared to trouble himself least with the details of government presided over a Council which was already utilizing the services of the expert and specialist. With the steady progress of English maritime enterprise, the creation of new institutions, the exigencies of two wars, and an awakening interest in the public conduct of the nation's affairs it came to be realized that the science of government is both complicated and difficult, dependent not only on the aptitude of its agents, but on the collection and interchange of intelligence. Already under the later Stuarts the foundations of a modern and efficient administration were being laid.

England in the Reign of Charles II, Clarendon Press (1934), 2nd edn, 1956, I, 189–90, 192, 194–7.

The King versus Commons

12 Betty Kemp, 1957

In the course of the period between the Restoration and the Reform Act there was achieved, and for a time maintained, a constitutional balance of power between a king who was still powerful, and a House of Commons which was newly powerful. The King's wooing of the Commons in this period was of pre-eminent importance because, since both were strong and neither was certainly ✳ sovereign, co-operation between them was essential. The fight between King and Commons in the seventeenth century restricted the King's powers without making the Commons his master, even in the financial sphere, and to contemporaries at least it was remarkable that the Commons remained so long content with an incomplete victory. Because they did, the relationship between King and Commons in the eighteenth century was, for the first and last time, a balanced relationship between two more or less equal partners, of which the second did not owe all its powers, nor indeed entirely its existence, to the first.

Because the Commons and the King's ministers were not, in practice, artificially bound together by the electorate, nor, in theory, bound together in any other way, the relationship of King and Commons dominated the whole of the period 1660–1832. The period began with an attempt to return, unconditionally, to the constitution as it was at the beginning of 1642, that is, to the old largely unwritten constitution as it had been modified by the early legislation of the Long Parliament. The attempt failed because it did not touch the problems which, in spite of this legislation, led to civil war and the abolition of kingship. The greatest of these problems was that of achieving co-operation between a king shorn of some of his prerogatives, and increasingly dependent financially on the Commons, and a House of Commons which, though aggressive and privileged, yet depended for its existence on the King. This problem was no nearer solution in 1660 than it was in 1642, and the next two reigns served only as a second commentary on the 1641 legislation. The uneasy co-operation of the first few years after the Restoration gave way, in the 1670s, to a series of charges by the Commons that the King was acting unconstitutionally, and before the end of Charles II's reign the Commons claimed, in the name of the constitution, the right to alter the succession and to prevent a Catholic from succeeding to the throne. The Commons failed to make good this claim only because their behaviour seemed, temporarily, to be more unconstitutional than the King's, and it was not long before James II, having succeeded to the throne in spite of his Catholicism, was opposed for his infringement of the constitution. The 1689 Revolution, by adding a good deal to the written constitution, reduced the size of the field within which it was possible for future kings to be unconstitutional. The reduction was taken further by the legislation of the next twenty-five years, which left no doubt that George I, a parliamentary king in a way in which William III had not been, was more and not less a king precisely because his title rested on parliamentary sanction and not on his own hereditary right. One of the ways in which parliament sought to confirm its right to make a king was by limiting the King's power to make a parliament, that is, to summon and dissolve one as he pleased. This was done, effectively and lastingly, by the Septennial Act of 1716, which marks the end of a period of constitutional definition. . . .

The separation of King and Commons, within the framework of a parliamentary monarchy, was foreshadowed when the Commons first claimed that their privileges were not dependent on the King, when they tried to restrict the King's exercise of his prerogative of summoning and dissolving parliament at his discretion, and when they asserted that they were a permanent part of the constitution. These claims by the Commons to independence of the King were more radical than either parliament's abolition of the monarchy or the Commons' abolition of the House of Lords, for they modified the constitution while the abolition of the monarchy and the House of Lords only suspended it. The restoration of the House of Lords in February 1660 by the recalled Rump, and the decision that a parliament of two Houses should meet, without the King's command, took the separation further. The Commons' agreement with the Lords, on 1 May 1660, that 'according to the ancient and fundamental laws of this Kingdom, the Government is and ought to be, by King, Lords and Commons', called Charles II back to the throne of his father. But the statement did not embody a recantation. Rather it was a statement of achievement: it replaced the old unity of 'King in Parliament' by the new trinity of 'King, Lords and Commons', and the replacement was perhaps only unchallenged because it was clothed in a restoration.

The period between 1660 and 1689 showed how limited the achievement was. It became clear in these years that the separation of King and Commons could have little meaning, in practice, while the Commons still depended for their existence entirely on the King, and while the King was not obliged by financial needs to have a parliament always in existence. At the same time, the theoretical separation of King and Commons presented more openly the problem of their normal relationship, a problem only intermittently recognized before 1660 and ignored in 1660. In some sense, of course, the problem of co-operation between the King and a House of Commons elected at his command and for the purpose of doing him service had always existed, but it was not an acute problem so long as King and Commons were so unequally matched that the phrase 'King in Parliament' was an accurate description of their normal relationship. By 1660 this was no longer true. Yet the Restoration confirmed the separation of King and Commons without in any way providing for co-operation between them. Indeed, it seemed that the Restoration was an attempt to combine a new theory with an old practice. The attempt failed, and could hardly have had more than temporary success. The Revolution of 1689 confirmed the new theory, and the Revolution settlement began to make the old practice impossible by imposing serious restrictions on the King's prerogative in relation to parliament. These restrictions had little connection with the Restoration; they were essentially the complement of the restrictions imposed by the Long Parliament in 1641, and they, rather than the Restoration, mark the real end of an interregnum. Even so, the achievement of 1689 was still negative: legal restrictions placed on a King who remained head of the executive could at best serve as a basis for co-operation between King and Commons, and the methods of co-operation between them remained to be worked out. But at least it can be said that the restrictions were an adequate basis for co-operation, since, though they bound the King so tightly that he could not again hope to be sovereign, they did not exalt the Commons to a position of sovereignty.

The restoration of the King in 1660 was unconditional....

In intention this was a return to the constitutional position of 1642 and a renewal of the attempt, which had then failed, to establish constitutional monarchy by imposing certain statutory limitations on the King. The attempt was based, as it had been in 1642, on the legislation of the first ten months of the Long Parliament, which had been primarily designed to define as unconstitutional, in the narrower sense of unlawful, the means by which Charles I had been enabled to rule for eleven years without summoning a parliament. This legislation was not referred to in 1660. Its validity, however, was indirectly confirmed by an Act of 1661 declaring void all later ordinances and orders—which had not received the royal assent—and making it a treasonable offence to state that either or both Houses of Parliament had 'a Legislative Power without the King'. None of the 1641 legislation was modified until 1664. The Triennial Act was then repealed and replaced by a new one, stating that a new parliament should be summoned within three years of a dissolution, but leaving the King to summon it. It could be contended, therefore, that Charles II implicitly accepted certain limitations on his prerogative: that he could not tax his subjects without parliament's consent, that justice could be dispensed only in the common law courts and in the court of Chancery, that he had no means of enforcing his proclamations, which could implement but not make law, and that intervals of more than three years between parliaments were unlawful and, until 1664, liable to be ended by the election and meeting of a parliament without the King's order. But, beyond the implicit acceptance of the position which had in 1642 heralded civil war, and of the fact that the King's prerogative could be limited by statute, the Restoration settled nothing. If the Civil War had been fought because the 1641 settlement was inadequate, then the Restoration settlement, which could hardly be regarded as less inadequate, was not more likely to be successful. The period it inaugurated was indeed little more than an experiment to see whether a later generation could get on better in circumstances which their fathers had found impossible.

For the House of Commons these circumstances involved the abandonment of Cromwell's reform of the franchise and redistribution of seats and a return to its old composition and structure. Here, at least, restoration proved not incompatible with progress: the last step in the transfer from King to Commons of control over the membership of the House was taken in the 1670s, when the Commons challenged the King's power to create new parliamentary boroughs and to define the right of election in them.

King and Commons, 1660–1832, Macmillan, 1957, pp. 1–10.

Executive versus Legislative Power

13   Clayton Roberts, 1966

At the opening of the civil war men had some conception of a balance of government, but none of the separation of powers.... The first man to describe the doctrine of the separation of powers in the language of Montesquieu and Blackstone was Sir John Wildman in *The Lawes Subversion*, which appeared in February 1648. Wildman wrote his pamphlet because Parliament imprisoned Sir John Maynard without showing cause. In *The Lawes Subversion* he argued that Maynard's imprisonment was illegal and indefensible because it was 'confounding the legislative power with the power judicial and executive of the laws...'. John Lilburne and his friends then put their trumpets to work popularizing this doctrine. In *The Agreement of the People* of December 1648 they urged 'that the Representative intermeddle not with the execution of laws, nor give judgment upon any man's person or estate...'. Though imprisoned and court martialed, they were still proclaiming five years later 'that Parliaments are not executioners of the law'. The framers of the Instrument of Government agreed in very few things with the Levellers, but they did agree in the necessity of separating the executive from the legislative power. The Instrument of Government placed legislative power in a Parliament and executive power in a Lord Protector and Council. The only written constitution in English history (like the American constitution) explicitly provided for the separation of legislative and executive powers....

By the year of the Restoration nearly everyone (but John Milton) agreed that in the separation of powers lay the 'grand secret of liberty and good government'. The Republican army officers who

occupied Whitehall in December 1659 declared it to be a fundamental law 'that the legislative and executive power be distinct
and not in the same hands'. The Long Parliament, clinging
desperately to power in January 1660, promised 'not to meddle'
with the execution of the law. Commonwealth men like Vane
and Harrington defended the doctrine. Royalists like Sir Roger
L'Estrange applauded it, and transmuted it into 'our old kingly
government'. 'Our old kingly government', L'Estrange wrote,
'included all the perfection of a free state, and was the kernel, as
it were, of a Commonwealth in the shell of Monarchy; the essential
parts of the Commonwealth are there, the Senate proposing, the
People resolving, and the Magistrate executing.' The people, he
asserted, possess the legislative power, the King the executive.

The principle of the separation of powers carried with it a collateral principle, the principle of checks and balances. The royalists
in 1660 found in this collateral principle the answer to the query
posed in 1648, *Quis custodit custodem?*. 'If the Commons are sovereign,' asked a royalist in the year of the Restoration, 'who will
be tribunes of the people to check them?...What is to prevent
then reiterated burdens on the people?...And who would prevent
a Parliament from arbitrarily arresting persons, as Parliament now
checks the King's arresting them so?' No one and nothing, he
answered; and the architects of the Restoration saw the point,
rejecting the idea of sovereignty in favour of a system of checks
and balances. As Colonel Gorges said in Parliament in 1659,
'The more checks, the better the constitution.'

Not least among the checks in this system of checks and balances
was the accountability of ministers to Parliament for their misuse
of the executive power. The gulf separating the legislative and
executive branches of government never grew so wide as to
destroy the principle of accountability, a fact which Sir Roger
L'Estrange admitted when he wrote that, we can never hope
'under our Commonwealth, whatever promises be made us, so
perfectly to distinguish the legislative from the ministerial authority
as once we did, when the House of Commons had not the power
of a Court leet to give an oath, nor of a Justice of Peace to make a
mittimus'. The King chooses his own ministers, he added, but alas
they are accountable to a triennial Parliament, 'which none but
[those of] the soundest integrity could abide'.

The principle of accountability survived the discredit cast on it by parliamentary misgovernment from 1640 to 1660. The principle may even have become more deeply rooted in English political life than before; and that for two reasons. First, those who advocated the principle found a doctrine for its philosophical justification that was more compelling than the doctrine of the twofold capacity of the King. This new doctrine taught that the people were the source of all political authority. John Locke had not yet given this doctrine its classic exposition, but it gained a wide currency in these years. Henry Parker taught that Parliament entrusts the King with power; John Wildman, Richard Overton, John Lilburne, and Sir Arthur Haselrigge proclaimed that all power resides originally in the people; Captain Baynes urged that 'the Council are trustees of the people'; and Sir Henry Vane and Thomas Scot maintained that the executive power is a gift which Parliament bestows on the Chief Magistrate. These radical men taught a radical doctrine, but it was also a useful one and therefore did not expire at the Restoration. If the people entrusted power to the King, their representatives in Parliament could call to account those to whom His Majesty then entrusted it.

The second reason why the principle of accountability grew in strength during these years concerns the habits of politicians, not their ideas. The constant exercise of the right of inquiry, of the right of interrogation, of the right of surveillance, of the right of criticism, and of the right of censure inculcated in members of Parliament habits that not even a Restoration could erase. During these years the two Houses of Parliament served an apprenticeship in the arts of superintending the executive. They questioned ministers of state. They clamoured for information. They objected to oaths of secrecy taken by their own committees. They sent committees of inquiry into the counties. They examined accounts and appropriated revenues. They investigated military failures and criticized naval designs. They opposed, condemned, criticized, and censured those whom they found remiss in the performance of their duties. Gradually they asserted a prescriptive right to these functions, and fell into habits that proved stronger than any philosophy of regal government.

The doctrine of the separation of powers and the principle of accountability were the two most enduring legacies of the Commonwealth period. Englishmen never again placed the executive power immediately in Parliament. Yet they never ceased criticizing in Parliament those to whom the King entrusted it. The line that men drew between a parliamentary executive and an executive accountable to Parliament was a fine one, but it was not an illogical one. Parliament knew what it wanted. It wanted to assume no responsibility, yet to continue to play the role of the critic. 'All the awe you have upon the King's Council hereafter', said the nameless member of the Convention Parliament in 1660, 'is, if they be such as the people have an ill opinion of, you may remove them, and it is better for us than to name them, for [then] we must be responsible for them.' This distinction holds true to this day. A party leader who can find a majority in the House of Commons may assume responsibility for the exercise of the executive power, but the House of Commons itself does not. Its members cling to the right to criticize, to question, to inquire, and to condemn.

It is no mere platitude that man cannot turn back the clock of history. Men may revive earlier forms of government and they may return to former allegiances, but they cannot cast off habits acquired over twenty years or dismiss predilections which they have unconsciously assumed. Englishmen before 1640 talked, as Miss Kemp observes, of the King *in* Parliament, men after 1660 of the King *and* Parliament.[1] Before 1640 there existed a unity of government, one King, who governed the realm by the advice of his judges, his Council, his nobility, and his faithful Commons. In 1660 there existed a balance of government, between the King with his prerogatives and Parliament with its privileges. At the centre of this balance lay a vague arrangement for the exercise of executive power. It should reside in the King, and not in the legislature. He should exercise it only after seeking the advice of Privy Councillors, whom he chose but in whom the nation confided. Their advices were advices, not commands. Yet these same councillors should answer to Parliament for the legality of their counsels, just as the King's officers should answer for the legality of their actions. If a councillor gave unlawful advice or a minister obeyed an unlawful command, the House of Commons could impeach and the House of Lords could try him. If the King employed councillors and ministers who were, though guilty of no crime, hateful to the people, Parliament could advise him to

[1] B. Kemp, *King and Commons*, 1957, p. 8.

dismiss them from office. But it could not take up arms to tear such persons from him.

This balance of government was not an absurd arrangement, nor was it inherently unworkable. It was not a utopian scheme, like Harrington's *Oceana*, but a product of hard-won experience.

The Growth of Responsible Government in Stuart England, Cambridge University Press, 1966, pp. 149–54.

Government in the Provinces

14 Christopher Hill, 1961

The Restoration of 1660 was a restoration of the united class whom Parliament represented, even more than of the King. The Convention Parliament was not summoned by the King; it summoned him. 'It is the privilege,... the prerogative of the common people of England,' Clarendon told the Lower House in 1661, 'to be represented by the greatest and learnedest and wealthiest and wisest persons that can be chosen out of the nation. ...The confounding the Commons of England...with the common people of England was the first ingredient into that accursed dose...a commonwealth.'...

A pamphlet of 1660 succinctly stated the position: 'This island ...is...governed by the influence of a sort of people that live plentifully and at ease upon their rents, extracted from the toil of their tenants and servants, each...of whom within the bounds of his own estate acts the prince.... They sit at the helm in the supreme council; they command in chief at sea and land; they impose taxes and levy it by commissioners of the same quality. Out of this rank select we sheriffs, Justices of Peace and all that execute the authority of a judge; by the influence of which powers they so order all elections, to Parliament or otherwise, that the whole counties follow their respective factions, and the common-alty in the votes are managed by them as the horse by his rider.' Parliamentary elections throughout the kingdom, Petty confirmed, 'are governed by less than 2,000 active men'. 'Acts of 1661–2 put the local levies of the militia under the King's control, but he had to act through Lords Lieutenant, who were of course the aristo-cracy. The latter nominated the leading county gentry as officers.

The duty of supplying horse and foot for the militia was based on a property qualification, higher in the case of cavalry. This ensured that the militia remained 'the fortress of liberty'. It had done much to restore Charles II in 1660....

Former Parliamentarians were at first little less determined than former Cavaliers that there should be no more trouble from the lower orders. The Act against Tumultuous Petitioning of 1661 forbade the collection of more than twenty signatures to a political petition to King or Parliament, 'unless the matter thereof have been first consented unto or ordered by three or more Justices of that county, or by the major part of the Grand Jury', or in London by Lord Mayor, aldermen, and common councillors. That would prevent anything like Leveller tactics of propaganda. It called the gentry in to redress the balance inside towns.

Century of Revolution, Nelson, 1961, pp. 222–3, 227.

15 Christopher Hill, 1967

The most important feature of the restoration for our purposes was its anti-democratic character. Lords came back to reinforce social snobbery, bishops to enforce religious inequality. The restoration put paid to the possibility of any extension of the franchise, any widening of the pale of the constitution. The extrusion of nonconformists from local government by the Clarendon Code intensified the dominance of the landed oligarchy and its hangers-on....

The breakdown of royal government had left the natural rulers of the countryside unmolested by the driving force of the Privy Council. During the interregnum, control of county committees had been seized by men of lesser rank, who did not shrink from radical measures, and this was followed by the rule of Cromwell's major-generals. But in 1660 the reunited gentry were left in complete control of the militia, the only effective armed force in the country, and of rural local government, with none of the supervision from Whitehall that Laud and the major-generals had exercised, though there were unpleasant moments under James II when nearly half the J.P.s in England and Wales were replaced and Judge Jeffreys tried to reassert the authority of the central government. J.P.s succeeded to many of the powers of the moribund church courts—e.g. in compelling the lower orders to attend church on Sundays. 'Now we may do what we will', a Quaker makes a J.P. say in 1660, 'and who shall control us?... Now will we build our decayed churches and restore our fallen worship: now will we repair the broken fences of our parks, that we may have game to the full.' In fact the iniquitous game laws date mainly from the restoration period. They established new privileges and disarmed the lower classes. An act of 1671 forbade anyone below the rank of £100 freeholder to kill 'game' on his own lands, and gave gamekeepers the right to enter and search houses of the lower orders, and to confiscate unauthorized weapons. During the civil war deer parks had been thrown open: soldiers and villagers had enjoyed unaccustomed feasts of venison. Many parks were never effectively restored: the gentry no longer confined hunting to their own land but chased the fox across country, regardless of ownership. The tyranny of the squire over his village, reinforced by the sycophancy of the parson, was virtually unchallenged for the remainder of our period. 'As J.P.s the gentry put down the riots of their labourers', wrote Mr Harding, 'and as M.P.s they passed the statutes which allowed them to do so.' 'The honour of being trusted and the pleasure of being feared', wrote Petty ironically in 1662, 'hath been thought a competent reward' for unpaid J.P.s. Sir John Oglander, more frankly, told his son that the office of J.P. was 'a place that may be a means to raise thy fortunes, being a place of gain'. All this did nothing to increase respect for the law among the lower classes.

Reformation to Industrial Revolution, Weidenfeld and Nicolson, 1967, pp. 110–11.

16   J.H. Plumb, 1967

The deep sense of independence, with its attendant suspicion of the Court, that ran through the Commons, was based on the position of the gentry and provincial merchants in local government. The extent of social, political, and judicial power in their hands was formidable; and behind this power lay the sanction of arms, for in the last resort they controlled the militia. As Sir Henry Capel told his fellow squires in the Commons in 1673, 'Our security is the militia: that will defend us and never conquer us'. Local royal officials, apart from the Lord-Lieutenants, had become nonentities, and the gentry, as Justices, bore the whole weight of administration. But their power was more extensive than this; they were very largely their own judges and, as Dawson has shown, judicial investigations and decisions that were properly a matter for Chancery were often delegated to them. Of course, they were subject to supervision: first Star Chamber, then Judges on Assize, could belabour them for incompetence, punish them for tyranny, and exhort them on behalf of the Crown. But only Cromwell and Charles II attempted to reduce their power; both failed. By 1688 the gentry were as deeply entrenched in their neighbourhoods as the baronage of Henry III. And they possessed a like intractable nature: both felt that, if the need arose, they had the right to rebel. The power of the seventeenth-century gentry was sanctioned by violence—riding out against their enemies, hamstringing their neighbour's dogs, beating their farmers' sons, or shooting down their riotous labourers. They played ducks and drakes with the law when it suited them, breaking with impunity what they were supposed to maintain. At Wigtown in 1708 the magistrates were involved with a large gang of smugglers who attacked and wounded the customs officers and seized a large cargo of brandy. Robert Walpole, a J.P. of Norfolk, had smugglers call regularly at his back door at Houghton and even used an Admiralty barge to run his wine up the Thames. He held government office at the time. Justices frequently closed alehouses for no other reason than that it drove custom to the one they owned themselves. Their quarrels, usually about rights of property, were frequent and bloody. A sea of turbulence washed about the gentry's lives, and they deeply resented any threat to the freedoms that they felt belonged to them as gentlemen. Since the days of the Tudors no government, royal or republican, had got to terms with them. Like Charles I or Charles II, Cromwell had failed absolutely to take the gentry into his control, and so made Restoration inevitable. Charles II's failure nearly toppled his throne. James II's was more complete; they chased him out of his kingdom. To bring the independent country gentry into some ordered relationship with government, or to diminish their role in it, became an absolute necessity if political stability was ever to be achieved....Parliament and the structure of local government were the key problems for centralizing monarchy.

The Growth of Political Stability in England, 1675–1725, Macmillan, 1967, pp. 20–2.

Town Government

17   The Duke of Newcastle, 1660

For Corporations. I see no reason why there should be so many, for why should tanners and shoemakers not be contented to be governed by the same way that lords, gentlemen, and good yeomen and freeholders are, which is by the known laws of the kingdom, by the judges and justices of peace. But these townsmen must be exempted by their charter. The truth is that every corporation is a petty free state against monarchy, and they have done your Majesty more mischief in these late disorders with their lecturers than anything else hath done.

Clarendon MS 109, f. 47, Bodleian Library, Oxford.

18   J.H. Sacret, 1930

One of the most familiar episodes of the latter part of the reign of Charles II, continued in that of his brother James II, is the general attack upon the charters of London and other cities and boroughs, and also various great corporations such as the London companies, the Inns of Court, the College of Physicians, the Universities, the Virginia company, and the New England colonies. The primary object of the policy, it is generally agreed, was that of securing control over elections to future parliaments; as well as that of gaining direct influence in the local government of the towns themselves. No doubt the Crown counted upon, and sometimes received, a measure of local support. The governing corporations in those days were generally exclusive, often negligent or even corrupt, and not infrequently at loggerheads with their fellow townsmen. The new charters sometimes conceded fresh privileges, such as additional fairs, and provisions for easier access to the ranks of freemen. But in spite of such attempts to make it palatable, the policy was too drastic an extension of the royal prerogative at the expense of ancient and cherished (albeit often abused) rights of municipal self-government to be other than generally unpopular; and its final and complete failure was signalized, when on the eve of the invasion of William of Orange, James II among other vain efforts to recover the alienated affections of his subjects issued a proclamation in October 1688 restoring to corporations 'their ancient charters, liberties, rights and franchises'. William's own declaration, at the same time, contained a similar phrase;...

At the Restoration of 1660 the position of most corporations must have been one of grave ambiguity, not to say danger. All had in fact condoned the usurpation. Many officials still held their places only in virtue of the Cromwellian charters, which the restored monarchy could not be expected to recognize, and many others only as a result of the still more questionable purges of the past years. Most, if not all, of the towns had compounded by lump sums for their fee-farm rents under the Commonwealth, and in this transaction again the Crown could not be expected to acquiesce... In their loyal addresses to the king, many of the corporations, making a virtue of necessity, voluntarily restored the fee-farm rents, not infrequently vouching that the latter had been purchased from the usurped authorities, only under dire necessity and in self-defence. Many, in the first flush of enthusiastic welcome, voted in addition generous gifts, which in some cases they had difficulty in meeting from their depleted resources, Norwich voting no less a sum than £1,000. And many of them petitioned at once or soon afterwards for renewal of their charters and confirmation of their ancient privileges....

... The government after the Restoration was actively engaged in establishing direct control over the corporations, not only by reinstatement of ejected royalists, but also by forced surrenders and remodellings of charters, by prerogative measures alone. It failed however to secure more than a part of its object, largely because of resistance, both local and parliamentary, on the ground of ancient privilege. More comprehensive powers therefore were necessary if the executive was to succeed in its object; and for these it was impelled to seek sanction from parliament itself. No serious difficulty was to be anticipated as yet from the county members. They were now loyalist to a man; and in the counties moreover the Crown possessed unhampered control over the appointment of all offices of dignity or profit, the lieutenancy, the sheriffs, the justices of the peace, and the militia. With the cities and boroughs, however, it was different. In the latter the appointment of these or similar officials belonged by charter almost invariably to the corporations alone; and most of them had also, either by charter or by prescription, the right to exclude all county officials from their precincts. Whilst it is true that many, if not most of the smaller boroughs were already falling under control of 'patrons', and normally returned country gentry as one or both of their members, even the latter had to consider the susceptibilities of their constituents when questions of chartered privilege were at issue. In the larger towns there was more often direct rivalry between the commercial magnates in control of the corporations and the landed interest of the county. Hence, whilst in pursuit of the policy now under discussion the Crown could count with reasonable confidence upon support in the counties, it was bound to regard developments in the towns with some apprehension, especially because with the rapid disbandment of the army during 1660 a strong republican influence was being restored to the resident population....

...The Corporation Act, or to give it its proper title, an Act for the well Governing and Regulating of Corporations [13 Car. II, stat. ii, c. 1] has scarcely received the attention it deserves, either from contemporary or modern writers....In modern works mention is generally made only of the clauses enforcing holders of municipal office to take the oaths of allegiance and supremacy and the oath of non-resistance to the king, to repudiate the solemn league and covenant, and to qualify for office by taking the sacrament. If, however, this unusually brief act of parliament be studied in full, it will be found that greater prominence is given to the following regulations. Until 25 March 1663 the administration of the act was to be in the hands of special commissioners nominated by the Crown, who were to have additional powers, besides those of exacting the oaths and declarations aforesaid. Any five or more of them, should they 'deem it expedient for the public safety', could by a majority remove from their offices any corporation officials, 'although such persons shall have taken and subscribed, or be willing to take and subscribe, the said oaths and declarations'. They were also empowered to fill up all vacancies thus created from among existing *or previous* inhabitants. . . . In other words, for the space of fifteen months the Crown was to have absolute control over the corporations, excluding and reappointing practically anybody it pleased. But even these powers fell far short of what the Crown seems to have sought, and probably would have achieved but for the opposition of the borough members in the house of commons. Apparently the court desired to make the commissioners' functions permanent instead of temporary, and to introduce immediately such drastic changes in the constitutions of the corporations that they would have become practically impotent or merely the tools of the executive.

. . . The measure finally agreed upon at the end of the session in December 1661 was apparently a compromise, and judging by further lists of amendments which fill more than three columns in the printed journal, the measure must have been almost entirely recast. The chief modifications seem to have been as follows: (i) These significant words were added to the preamble,

It being too well known, that notwithstanding all his Majesty's Endeavours, and unparalleled Indulgence, in pardoning all that is passed; nevertheless, many evil Spirits are still working: Wherefore, for Prevention of the like Mischief for the Time to come, and for Preservation of the Publick Peace, both in Church and State . . .

(ii) The commons lost the right, which they had claimed, of nominating the commissioners to administer the act; this was left in the hands of the Crown under the Great Seal. (iii) The commissioners so nominated were, however, to retain those stringent and arbitrary powers against which Prynne had especially protested, and which have been so frequently overlooked by modern historians. (iv) Probably as a result of the reappearance of the bishops in the house of lords a proviso was added imposing further the well-known sacramental test for municipal office. The commons indeed managed to secure some concessions: (i) the more

drastic amendments of the lords, requiring renewal or surrender
of all charters, Crown nomination of officials, and the intervention
of county justices in towns, were not insisted upon; (ii) corporation
charters were to be indemnified against forfeiture by reason of
any misdeed or lapse committed before the first day of the parliament (8 May 1661); and (iii) the powers of the special royal
commissioners were to terminate on 25 March 1663; only after
that date administration of the act was to be left, in the first place,
to the town officials or justices; though if the latter failed to act,
the detested county justices were then empowered to intervene.
But, even making allowance for these concessions, it is evident
that for the space of over a year municipal charters were virtually
suspended, and in the interval the Crown had practically unlimited
right to revolutionize the personnel of the corporations throughout
the land.... Although it was clearly against the interests of the
Crown to create unnecessary antagonism even in these reputed
'nests of sedition', there is ample evidence to be found, even in
the usual printed sources, that these powers were drastically
utilized. The commissions were nearly always composed of the
leading royalist country gentry of the several counties under the
presidency of the lords lieutenant. Apart from necessary technical
advisers such as stewards or recorders, townsmen themselves
were generally ignored, it being obviously impracticable, as
Marvell had naively remarked to his constituents, that 'the same
should be judges and judged'.

'The Restoration Government and the municipal corporations',
English Historical Review, XLV, 1930, pp. 232, 237–8, 245–7, 250–2.

Part Two

THE RELIGIOUS SETTLEMENT:
National Policy and Local Solutions
National policy

To contemporaries on the eve of the Restoration the reinstatement of the bishops was certainly not a foregone conclusion. General Monk's speech in the House of Commons in February, 1660 (19), and John Price's report of his conversation with Monk in the same month (20) illustrates the indecision of one influential personality. Dr (later Bishop) Burnet recorded in his *History of My Own Time* (21) events in which he played no influential part, but of which he received accounts from others who did. He was at court for a great part of the years 1662–4. He desired a religious settlement which would concede toleration to all religious creeds, and he believed that this was the majority view in the early days of the Restoration: according to him Clarendon favoured it because of the half promises made by Charles II; Charles II favoured it because he wanted to keep the way open for a return to Catholicism. But things turned out differently. Burnet placed much blame on Richard Baxter at the Savoy conference for his wearisome 'logical arguing' which alienated many men who were friendly to the Presbyterians. He also attributed considerable influence to those with Catholic sympathies who favoured a policy of extreme intolerance towards Puritans in the belief that only through the experience of persecution could men be persuaded how desirable was toleration for all, even for Catholics. In the long run, the latter view proved right in the sense that persecution turned public opinion against the policy and in favour of toleration. But did hindsight lead Burnet to lay so much emphasis on this point of view? His *History* was written some years after the events he describes.

Richard Baxter also conceded that the Anglicans at the beginning genuinely desired toleration and that the Worcester House Declaration was sincerely intended (22). But his account of the

37

Savoy conference shows only too clearly how he alienated some of the bishops by his verbosity and stickling logic. He also received harsh criticism from the Independents for his handling of the negotiations, though he claimed that they later exonerated him when they heard the full story.

Recent writers on the religious settlement at the Restoration consider that, although Charles II returned to England without conditions, certain issues were already decided. The alliance forged between the king and Anglican churchmen in exile, for example, meant that the restoration of episcopacy was never in doubt. They differ in their views on the sincerity with which different religious groups and different individuals strove for a comprehensive Church in the spirit of the Declaration of Breda. They agree that the final separation of Anglicans from Dissenters, considered from the national standpoint, was a tragedy although they differ on whether the outcome was inevitable.

Dr Bosher's detailed study suggests that leading Anglicans followed a consistent and carefully calculated strategy which, in three phases of negotiation, neatly achieved their chosen objective. The Church of England was established as a broad church, but firm and clear bounds were set to its comprehensiveness. His verdict is the more generous because he judges comprehension and the settlement of 1662 as a separate issue from toleration and the later persecuting acts of the Clarendon Code, the Conventicle and Five-Mile Acts. He justifies this partly by hindsight and partly by the choice of 1662 as the terminal date of his study (23). The controversy over comprehension was settled permanently in 1662, while the policy of intolerance towards dissenters did not develop its full rigour until after 1662, and it lasted in its full severity for less than thirty years. Other writers tend to pass judgment on the settlement of 1662 in the light of the policies adopted between 1664 and 1665.

Dr Whiteman sees more empiricism in Anglican tactics (24). In the course of their negotiations with the Presbyterians between 1660 and 1662 the Anglicans were gradually encouraged to take a firmer stand by the shift of public opinion in their favour, even while they continued to hope and work for a compromise agreement. She deems the outcome 'a tragedy' which involved much human suffering, and apportions the blame evenly between the parties.

The apparent and real attitudes of the leading personalities in the negotiations are much debated, particularly those of Charles II, Clarendon, Gilbert Sheldon, Bishop of London, and Richard Baxter, the Puritan divine. Not all their motives and opinions can be readily discovered. Most writers come round to the view that recent events were too fresh in the memory, and fears for the future pacification of the kingdom loomed too large to permit a compromise settlement satisfactory to all. But there are differences of view on where the deepest divisions lay, whether between the Anglicans and Presbyterians, between the Presbyterians and Independents, or within the ranks of the Anglican Church between the Laudians and the Episcopalians.

Local Solutions

While the Church settlement was made at Westminster, and an Anglican Church was reinstated, backed by strong state support in enforcing a policy of religious uniformity, the tone of that policy was determined by the spontaneous reactions of people in their own localities. They in the end passed the final verdict. The religious settlement at the local level was at least as important as the history of policy-making at the centre, but it has been the least explored.

Some churchmen thought it would be easy to secure uniformity in the nation if once the parson led the way. They could not envisage Dissent remaining a permanent force in English religious life. Richard Baxter on the other hand was astonished at such a viewpoint and could not imagine how the teachings of the Church could possibly convert his parishioners from Puritan to orthodox Anglican views. He gives an unfriendly account of the tactics used by the Anglican clergy to win over their Puritan-minded congregations (25). Clearly the path was not easy. In some parishes no minister was presented in place of the deprived clergy: the Bishop of Exeter explains why John Quick, in consequence of this situation, shortly returned to minister to his flock at Brixton in Devon, though he was not allowed to stay long (26). By 1677 official policy was being rejected by most country people (27).

In many places the gentry were powerful allies of the parson and strengthened his hand at an early stage. Some justices of the peace, indeed, marched ahead of the government in restoring the old order of things between 1660 and 1662. They were mostly gentry with the clear intention of sweeping away all traces of the recent past. Dr Bosher admits the hardening attitude of intolerance among the ruling class (28), but excuses the government on the grounds that it was obliged to recognize in these zealous, gentlemanly upholders of the monarchy and the Anglican Church its chief allies, and to lean on them more heavily, because discontent among the dissenters seemed to pose a continual threat to the new regime. Dr Hill describes the corresponding hardening of opinion among those excluded from the English Church (29). They withdrew into a world where religion did not disable them. This had important consequences for economic life, the more so since many dissenters also became geographically segregated in definable rural and urban industrial areas.

G.M. Trevelyan describes in eloquent and imaginative prose the widening social gulf between conformists and Nonconformists (30). He also puts clearly and unequivocally a not uncommon opinion that the effects of intolerance, seen in long perspective, were beneficial. In this long perspective too he notices how some puritan attitudes in English life persisted into the twentieth century, despite their rejection in 1660 by the official Church (31). William Haller presents another optimistic view of the religious settlement, but expresses it in still more positive terms: great creative energies were released by the cleavage in religious life between Anglicans and Dissenters (32). At this point, however, it is perhaps necessary to reread Douglas Lacey's reminder that the division of religious opinion between conformity and dissent was not as clear cut as these conclusions imply. The two groups spanned many fine shades of opinion that merged into one another (33).

Dr Whiteman underlines the conservatism of the restoration in its administrative aspects, and stresses its far-reaching consequences (34). The Church kept its parsons poor and ineffective in their parishes, while it enriched its bishops. By reviving its disciplinary courts in their old form, it made them the butt of popular resentment, and the Church lost its influence on the social life of local communities. It thus had little resistance to offer to the growth of Methodism in the eighteenth century.

Episcopacy or Presbytery?

19   General Monk, 1660

Speech in the House of Commons, 21 February 1660

As to a government in the Church, the want whereof hath been no small cause of these nations' distractions, it is most manifest that if it be monarchical in the State, the Church must follow, and prelacy must be brought in, which these nations I know cannot bear, and against which they have so solemnly sworn. And indeed moderate not rigid Presbyterian government, with a sufficient liberty for consciences truly tender, appears at present to be the most indifferent and acceptable way to the church's settlement.

The Parliamentary or Constitutional History of England by Several Hands, 1760, XXII, p. 142.

20   John Price, 1660

*Price was Monk's chaplain and confidant
at the Restoration*

He [Monk] detained me with this serious discourse upon the thing [the restoration of the bishops], that he thought this could never be done, for *not only their lands are sold* (says he) *but the temper of the nation is against them.* I told him that as yet he could not see the temper of the nation; the royal party having judged it prudence not to appear openly, or make any addresses. But since he had mentioned it, I entreated him to grant me one request; which was that he would not be drawn to engage against them; and this I thought he might safely grant me now, who would not be ensnared to abjure the king and the royal family. He paused a while (as his manner was) and taking me by the hand, Well then (said he), *so much I will promise you that I will not be engaged against bishops.* I thanked him and kissed his hand, adding that it was best to leave it to God's providence and the next Parliament, when we should be able to discern the temper of the nation in reference both to church and state.

The Mystery and Method of His Majesty's Happy Restauration laid open to Public View, 1680, pp. 117–18.

21   Bishop Burnet, *c.* 1700

The first point in debate was, whether concessions should be made, and pains taken to gain the dissenters, or not; especially the presbyterians. The earl of Clarendon was much for it; and got the king to publish a declaration soon after his Restoration concerning ecclesiastical affairs, to which if he had stood, very probably the greatest part of them might have been gained. But the bishops did not approve of this: and after the service they did that lord in the Duke of York's marriage, he would not put any hardship on those who had so signally obliged him. This disgusted the Lord Southampton, who was for carrying on the design that had been much talked of during the wars, of moderating matters both with relation to the government of the church, and the worship and ceremonies: which created some coldness between him and the earl of Clarendon, when the lord chancellor went off from those designs. The consideration that those bishops and their party had in the matter was this: the presbyterians were possessed of most of the great benefices in the church, chiefly in the city of London, and in the two universities. It is true, all that had come into the room of those who were turned out by the parliament, or by the visitors sent by them, were removed by the course of law, as men that were illegally possessed of other men's rights: and that, even where the former incumbents were dead, because a title originally wrong was still wrong in law. But there were a great many of them in very eminent posts, who were legally possessed of them.

Many of these, chiefly in the city of London, had gone into the design of the Restoration in so signal a manner, and with such success, that they had great merit, and a just title to very high preferment. Now, as there remained a great deal of the old animosity against them, for what they had done during the wars, so it was said, it was better to have a schism out of the church than within it; and that the half-conformity of the puritans before the war, had set up a faction in every city and town between the lecturers and the incumbents; that the former took all methods to render themselves popular, and to raise the benevolence of their people, which was their chief subsistence, by disparaging the government both in church and state. They had also many stories among them, of the credit they had in the elections of Parliament men, which they infused in the king, to possess him with the necessity of having none to serve in the church, but persons that should be firmly tied to his interest, both by principle, and by subscriptions and oaths. It is true, the joy then spread through the nation had got at this time a new Parliament to be elected, of men so high and so hot, that unless the court had restrained them, they would have carried things much farther than they did, against all that had been concerned in the late wars: but they were not to expect such success at all time: therefore they thought it was necessary to make sure work at this time: and, instead of using methods to bring in the sectaries, they resolved rather to seek the most effectual ones for casting them out, and bringing a new set of men into the church. This took with the king, at least it seemed to do so. But though he put on an outward appearance of moderation, yet he was in another and deeper laid design, to which the heat of these men proved subservient, for bringing in of popery. A popish queen was a great step to keep it in countenance at court, and to have a great many priests going about the court making converts. It was thought, a toleration was the only method for setting it a going all the nation over. And nothing could make a toleration for popery pass, but the having great bodies of men put out of the church, and put under severe laws, which should force them to move for a toleration, and should make it reasonable to grant it to them. And it was resolved, that whatever should be granted of that sort should go in so large a manner, that papists should be comprehended within it. So the papists had this generally spread among them, that they should oppose all propositions for comprehension, and should animate the church party to maintain their ground against all the sectaries. And in that point they seemed zealous for the church. But at the same time they spoke of toleration, as necessary both for the peace and quiet of the nation, and for the encouragement of trade. And with this the duke was so possessed, that he declared himself a most violent enemy to comprehension, and as zealous for toleration. The king being thus resolved on fixing the terms of conformity to what they had been before the war, without making the least abatement or alteration, they carried on still an appearance of moderation, till the strength of the parties should appear in the new parliament.

[At the Savoy conference,] the two men, that had the chief management of the debate, were the most unfit to heal matters, and the fittest to widen them that could have been found out. Baxter was the opponent, and Gunning was the respondent... Baxter and he spent some days in much logical arguing, to the diversion of the town, who thought here were a couple of fencers engaged in disputes, that could never be brought to an end, nor have any good effect. In conclusion, this commission being limited to such a number of days, came to an end, before any one thing was agreed on. The bishops insisted on the laws that were still in force, to which they would admit of no exception, unless it was proved that the matter of those laws was sinful. They charged the presbyterians with having made a schism, upon a charge against the church for things, which now they themselves could not call sinful. They said, there was no reason to gratify such a sort of men in anything; one demand granted would draw on many more: all authority both in church and state was struck at by the position they had insisted on, that it was not lawful to impose things indifferent, since they seemed to be the only proper matter in which human authority could interpose. So this furnished an occasion to expose them as enemies to all order. Things had been carried at the Savoy with great sharpness, and many reflections. Baxter said once, such things would offend many good men in the nation. Stearn, the archbishop of York, upon that took notice that he would not say kingdom, but nation, because he would not acknowledge a king. Of this great complaints were made, as an indecent return for the zeal they had shewn in the restoration.

The conference broke up without doing any good. It did rather hurt, and heightened the sharpness that was then in people's minds to such a degree, that it needed no addition to raise it higher.... The Act [of Uniformity, 1662] passed by no great majority: and by it, all who did not conform to the liturgy by the twenty-fourth of August, St Bartholomew's Day, in the year 1662, were deprived of all ecclesiastical benefices, without leaving any discretional power with the king in the execution of it, and without making provision for the maintenance of those who should be so deprived: a severity neither practised by Queen Elizabeth in the enacting her liturgy, nor by Cromwell in ejecting the royalists, in both which a fifth part of the benefices was reserved for their subsistence. St Bartholomew's Day was pitched on, that, if they were then deprived, they should lose the profits of the whole year, since the tithes are commonly due at Michaelmas. The presbyterians remembered what a St Bartholomew's had been held at Paris ninety years before, which was the day of that massacre, and did not stick to compare the one to the other. The Book of Common Prayer with the new corrections was that to which they were to subscribe: but the corrections were so long a preparing, and the vast number of copies, above two thousand, that were to be wrought off for all the parish churches of England, made the impression go on so slowly, that there were few books set out to sale when the day came. So, many that were affected to the church, but that made conscience of subscribing to a book that they had not seen, left their benefices on that very account. Some made a journey to London on purpose to see it. With so much precipitation was that matter driven on, that it seemed expected that the clergy should subscribe implicitly to a book they had never seen. This was done by too many, as I was informed by some of the bishops: but the presbyterians were now in great difficulties; they had many meetings, and much disputing about conformity. Reynolds accepted of the bishopric of Norwich: but Calamy and Baxter refused the sees of Lichfield and Hereford. And about two thousand of them fell under the parliamentary deprivation, as they gave out. The numbers have been much controverted. This raised a grievous outcry over the nation, though it was less considered at that time than it would have been at any other. Baxter told me that had the terms of the king's declaration been stood to, he did not believe that above three hundred of these would have been so deprived. Some few, and but few, of the episcopal party were troubled at this severity, or apprehensive of the very ill effects it was like to have. Here were many men, much valued, some on better grounds, and others on worse, who were now cast out ignominiously, reduced to great poverty, provoked by much spiteful usage, and cast upon those popular practices that both their principles and their circumstances seemed to justify, of forming separate congregations, and of diverting men from the public worship, and from considering their successors as the lawful pastors of those churches in which they had served. The blame of all this fell heaviest on Sheldon. The earl of Clarendon was charged with his having entertained the presbyterians with hopes and good words, while he was all the while carrying on, or at least giving way, to the bishop's project....

He [Peter Welsh, a Franciscan priest] told me often, there was nothing which the whole popish party feared more than an union of those of the church of England with the presbyterians; they knew we grew the weaker, the more our breaches were widened; and that the more we were set against one another, we would mind them the less. The papists had two maxims, from which they never departed: the one was to divide us, and the other was to keep themselves united, and either to set on an indiscriminated toleration, or a general prosecution; for so we loved to soften the harsh word of persecution. And he observed, not without great indignation at us for our folly, that we, instead of uniting among ourselves, and dividing them, according to their maxims, did all we could to keep them united, and to disjoint our own body.

Bishop Burnet s History of His Own Time, 1857 edn, pp. 121–4, 126, 134.

22   Richard Baxter, 1696

Yet I think that those men are reproveable who say that nothing but deceit and juggling was from the beginning intended, for who knoweth other men's intents but God? Charity requireth us to think that they speak nearer to the truth who say that, while the diocesan doctors were at Breda, they little dreamt that their way to their highest grandeur was so fair, and, therefore, that then they would have been glad of the terms of the Declaration of Breda; and that when they came in, it was necessary that they should proceed safely, and feel whether the ground were solid under them, before they proceeded to their structure. The land had been but lately engaged against them. The Covenant had been taken even by the lords and gentlemen of their own party at their composition. There was the army that brought them in (who were Presbyterians as to the most of the ruling part) to be disbanded. And how knew they what the Parliament would do? Or that there would be none to contest against them in the Convocation? How could they know these things beforehand? Therefore it was necessary that moderate things should be proposed and promised, and no way was so fit as by a declaration, which being no law, is a temporary thing, giving place to laws. And it was needful that the calling of a synod were delayed till the Presbyterians were partly cast out, and a way to keep out the rest secured. And if when all these things were done, the former promises were as the Independents called the Covenant, like an almanac out of date, and if severities were doubled in comparison of what they were before the wars, no man can wonder that well understood the persons and the causes.

[In the discussions at the Savoy conference] I went on and told him [Dr Gunning] that I also granted that a man for a certain space might be without any act of sin; and as I was proceeding, here Bishop Morley interrupted me, according to his manner, with vehemency, crying out, 'What can any man be for any time without sin!' And he sounded out his aggravations of this doctrine; and then cried to Dr Bates, 'What say you, Dr Bates, is this your opinion?' Saith Dr Bates, 'I believe that we are all sinners; but I pray, my lord, give him leave to speak.' I began to go on to the rest of my sentence where I left, to shew the sense and truth of my words; and the bishop (whether in passion or design I know not) interrupted me again, and mouthed out the odiousness of my doctrine again and again. I attempted to speak, and still he interrupted me in the same manner. Upon that I sat down and told him that this was neither agreeable to our commission, nor the common laws of disputation, nor the civil usage of men in common converse, and that if he prohibited me to speak, I desired him to do it plainly, and I would desist, and not by that way of interruption. He told me I had speaking enough if that were good, for I spake more than anyone in the company. And thus he kept me so long from uttering the rest of my sentence that I sat down, and gave over and told him I took it for his prohibition.

I oft made it my earnest request to them but that we might have our proper turns in speaking, and that we might not interrupt one another, but stay the end. But I could never prevail, especially with Bishop Morley, who, when anything was spoken which he would not have to be spoken out, would presently interrupt me, and go on in his way. I told them that if they took this course, I judged all our conference fruitless to the hearers, for my speeches were not incoherent, but the end and middle must be joined to the beginning to make up the sense, and that as the end is first in the intention, but last in execution, so I usually reserved the chief part of what I had to say to the last, to which the beginning was the preparatory. And therefore I had rather they forbad me to speak any more than let me begin and then not suffer me to go on any further. The bishop answered that I spake so long, and had so many things, that their memories could not retain them all, and should lose the first if they stayed till the last; and that I spake more than any other. I told him that as to my speaking more than others, it was my duty, yea, to speak as much as all the rest, except when my brethren saved me that labour. If they thought I spake too much, they would tell me so. And for others, one side was to speak as oft as the other side.

[*Some of the Presbyterians' official papers, compiled in answer to the bishops' and the king's proposals, were published without authority, most of them, said Baxter,* 'by some poor men for gain, without our knowledge and correction, ...so falsely printed that our wrong by it is very great'.]

The coming forth of these papers had various effects: it increased the burning indignation which before was kindled against me on one side, and it somewhat mitigated the censures that were taken up against me on the other side. For you must know that the chief of the Congregational (or Independent) party took it ill that we took not them with us in our treaty, and so did a few of the Presbyterian divines. All whom we so far passed by as not to invite them to our councils (though they were as free as we to have done the like) because we knew that it would be but a hindrance to us, partly because their persons were unacceptable, and partly because it might have delayed the work. And most of the Independents, and some few Presbyterians, raised it as a common censure against us, that if we had not been so forward to meet the bishops with the offers of so much at first, and to enter a treaty with them without just cause, we had all had better terms, and standing off would have done more good. So that, though my person and intentions had a more favourable censure from them than some others, yet for the action I was commonly censured by them as one that had granted them too much, and wronged my brethren by entering into this treaty, out of too earnest a desire of concord with them. Thus were men on both extremes offended with me, and I found what enmity, charity, and peace are like to meet with in the world. But when these papers were printed, the Independents confessed that we had dealt faithfully and satisfactorily. And indifferent men said that reason had overwhelmed the cause of the diocesans, and that we had offered them so much as left them utterly without excuse. And the moderate episcopal men said the same. But the engaged prelatist were vehemently displeased that these papers should thus come abroad.

Matthew Sylvester, *Reliquiae Baxterianae, or Mr Richard Baxter's Narrative of the most Memorable Passages of his Life and Times*, 1696, pp. 287–8, 337, 339, 379–80.

The Making of the Settlement: National Policy in Perspective

23   Robert S. Bosher, 1957

Some mystery still attaches to the ecclesiastical settlement of the Restoration. Its uncompromising character stands in marked contrast to the spirit of moderation which prevailed in other matters at issue. The political policy adopted by Edward Hyde was generous and conciliatory, and early signs indicated that a similar line would be followed in dealing with the Puritans. Various plans were sponsored for remodelling the Church in the interests of comprehensiveness, and men remembered that the Royalist party in the past had shown little sympathy to High Church pretensions. Despite this beginning, the second year of the Restoration saw the triumph of a militant High Anglicanism in the Establishment, and the final exclusion of all the nonconforming clergy....

The events which led to this dénouement form a pattern which is inconsistent and puzzling, and the original intentions of the Royalist statesmen and clergy have never been satisfactorily determined. First-hand evidence is scanty and open to different interpretations; as a result, the judgments of historians have varied according to their prepossessions. Anglican writers have tended to telescope the progressive stages of the settlement, and to suggest that the restoration of the old Church followed automatically on the King's return, supported by a wave of Anglican sentiment throughout the nation. Nonconformist historians have simplified the story no less drastically, appealing for justification to two standard sources—Baxter's memoirs and Clarendon's autobiography. In their version, the Royalist government and Anglican clergy were united from first to last in a determination to drive Puritans from the Establishment, and the attempts at conciliation were a means of temporizing until the end could be achieved. More recently, a third view has been advanced—that the Chancellor was essentially an Anglican latitudinarian, desiring to unite the conservative religious parties in a comprehensive State Church. On this theory, the negotiations with the Presbyterians were entirely *bona fide*, and were only frustrated by the obstinacy of the bishops and the anti-Puritan violence of the old Cavaliers. . . .

The foundations of the Laudian triumph were firmly laid during the years of the Interregnum. In 1649, when the strong hand of Oliver Cromwell gave order to the nation, Anglicans faced the problem of adjustment to a new régime, the outcome of successful revolution in Church and State. The Protector's leniency during the first years of his rule made possible the rallying of a movement which had been thoroughly shattered by the measures of a Puritan Parliament. . . .

The Laudian party represented that section of Anglicanism which could not be assimilated in any general union of Protestants. The essentially Catholic interpretation of the Anglican settlement had deeply influenced the younger church leaders, and these men opposed Cromwell's programme on theological as well as political grounds. Circumstances combined to give the Laudians a clear field as spokesmen of the Anglican tradition. They alone could claim full loyalty to the Church of England as it had formerly existed, and unlike their conforming brethren, they had no motive to temper zeal with discretion in their propaganda for the old faith. The refusal of the surviving bishops to accept responsibility and assume spiritual jurisdiction ended the hope that the various types of Anglicans might preserve a corporate unity, and leadership therefore passed to the men whose aims were consistent and aggressive; and who would risk danger and persecution to achieve them. So completely did the High Church group become identified with Anglican resistance that it lost consciousness of being an ecclesiastical party, and saw itself as 'the faithful remnant of the old Church of England'.

Laudian policy was not so much calculated as instinctive—to commend Anglicanism as the religious aspect of the Royalist creed, and to stake the future of the Church of England on a restoration of the monarchy. . . . Loyalty to the King was taught as a religious duty, and the clergy who remained in England were always ready to act as political agents. In various ways this uncompromising Royalism served to re-establish the fortunes of the old High Church party. Intimate relations were formed with the exiled Court, and a strong claim laid on the future favour and gratitude of the King. A new and stronger sense of churchmanship among the Cavalier gentry was their natural reaction to the Puritan attack on the Church, and this temper was assiduously fostered by the tracts and theological works of the Laudian clergy. As chaplains and tutors in Royalist households, these divines implanted in the younger generation a fervent devotion to the Church, gaining for High Church principles a source of political strength hitherto lacking.

If the Laudians in England made capital of their loyalty to the Crown, it remained for another group to ensure the Crown's continued support of the Church. The clergy who sought refuge in exile were almost exclusively of the High Anglican school, and kept in close touch with their friends at home. During the years when a pro-Anglican policy seemed more of a hindrance than an advantage to the Royalist cause, these men worked to defeat the counsels which urged on the young King either a Presbyterian or a Roman Catholic alliance. Charles's treaty with the Scots in 1650 was a heavy blow, but after the defeat at Worcester the following year, the Anglican party rapidly regained its influence. Henceforth, Hyde, Nicholas, and Ormond were the counsellors to whom the King chiefly deferred, and they were on terms of intimacy with the exiled clergy. Their insistence that the Royalist programme called for a return to the old Constitution carried with it the corollary that the Church should recover her ancient rights, and on this point logic was reinforced by strong devotion to the Anglican tradition. Divines like Cosin, Morley, and Bramhall were active in promoting this spirit among the refugees, and by a confident vindication of the Anglican position they largely frustrated Romanist attempts to absorb the forlorn remnant of the English Church. At the close of the Interregnum, they had good reason for satisfaction—Royalist policy was controlled by men who regarded the interests of Crown and Church as inseparable....

With Monk's rise to power, and the emergence of the Presbyterian party as a vital factor in plans for a Restoration, the religious question became acute. An avowal of an Anglican policy by the exiled government was seen to be impracticable, and Charles took refuge in vague promises of toleration and a future settlement by Parliament.... The evasive tactics of the Anglicans, aided by Monk's pressure for an unconditional Restoration, enabled the Royalist government to assume power in May, 1660, unhampered by any concrete engagement to the Presbyterians.

...At a time when confusion and uncertainty reigned in England, and no man dared predict what the next turn of events might bring, it would indeed be misleading to imply that the negotiations directed by Hyde were one step in a far-sighted and carefully planned strategy—a great 'conspiracy', as the Puritans were later to charge. The Anglicans were no more prescient than others; but through all the changes of the Spring, they continued to give proof of that consistency of principle and resistance to compromise which they had shown throughout the Interregnum. However opportunist its tactics, the Laudian party never lost sight of the final goal—complete restoration of the old Church. Two factors in particular combined to make this policy effective; the intransigence of the Laudian divines, determined to secure all or nothing in the religious settlement, and the statesmanship of Hyde, who was able to cloak this aim with a wise and cautious diplomacy....

By May, 1661, the re-establishment of the Church of England was, in all essentials, virtually complete. Within a year of the Restoration, the plan of Hyde and his clerical allies had been consummated; the Church had recovered by degrees what could not be had at once. The role of Parliament in this work had been merely negative—the refusal, after a prolonged internal struggle, to take a hand in the church settlement. But this very act of renunciation was an achievement of the Laudian party. Only one reverse had marked the gradual reconstruction of the old ecclesiastical order. The Act for Settling Ministers had overridden traditional Anglican requirements, and given legal tenure in the Establishment to clergy who would formerly have been debarred. As one looks back, the course of events seems at first sight to have been governed by a confused interplay between an official policy of conciliation and an instinctive movement of religious reaction. But if the story has been correctly interpreted, it is possible to discern an intelligible plan of action. Three separate crises mark the stages of Anglican advance, and each was accompanied by a similar reaction on the part of the government.

In June, 1660, the Royalists assumed power, well aware that the

Restoration was partly due to Presbyterian influence. The religious sentiment of the country was uncertain, and the stability of the new regime far from assured. Negotiations for a comprehensive church settlement were therefore undertaken with Presbyterian leaders. The proclamation against forcible ejections, the appointment of Presbyterian chaplains, and the King's non-committal attitude towards the bishops were meant to reassure the Puritan party. Under cover of this feigned conciliation, the government proceeded at once to the first stage of its programme—the filling of strategic posts in the Establishment with the Laudian clergy, and the restoring of cathedral chapters preparatory to the election of bishops.

In the late summer, a new crisis arose, due largely to the steady encroachment of Anglicans on the Establishment, and to the consequent alarm of the Puritans. When negligence on the part of churchmen enabled the Presbyterian party to gain control of the House of Commons, strenuous efforts were made to protect the Puritan incumbents, climaxing in a scarcely veiled attack on the Court's ecclesiastical appointments. The government resorted to the same strategy as before, first obtaining a breathing spell by adjourning Parliament. Friendly negotiations were resumed with the Puritans, and public announcement made of a satisfactory settlement; the Royal Declaration was designed both to soothe the Puritans, and forestall further action by Parliament in the matter of religion. Preferment was also offered to leaders of the opposition. But once again, these measures were a strategic diversion for a further Anglican advance. Before the end of the recess, the restoration of episcopacy along the old lines was well under way, and pressure was being exerted on the parish clergy to comply with the old laws. This time the Puritans were not so easily reassured, and in a crucial struggle in the House of Commons the Church party was barely able to frustrate their counter-measure— the attempt to give the Royal Declaration [i.e. the Worcester House Declaration] legal force.

By March, 1661, indignation at the steady restoration of Anglican discipline had again reached a boiling point in the capital. The Guildhall election was an alarming proof of religious discontent, and for the third time the government hastened to relieve the tension by a conciliatory gesture. Within a week the warrant for the Savoy Conference was being perused by Londoners. But as before, the tender of a compromise settlement was not allowed to delay the progress of re-establishment. No sooner had fear of danger subsided than the Convocations were summoned to assemble in traditional manner, and the administrative machinery of the Church of England was at last fully operative.

This, in bare outline, is the strategy by which the Laudian party and its sympathizers achieved success within so brief a period, and disposed of the formidable problem of Puritan opposition. Admittedly, certain episodes in the story, seen apart from the context of the long-term policy, may be made to bear a different interpretation. For example, conclusive evidence of Hyde's state of mind in October, 1660, is not available; since human policy is always subject to inconsistency and unpredictable deviations, some historians have believed that the Chancellor and even the Laudian clergy were at that moment genuinely desirous of a comprehensive church settlement. But a considerable body of indirect evidence suggests strongly that never at any time was the government prepared to give security for its generous proposals; the favour it showed the Puritans was mostly in words, whereas the Anglicans profited steadily by its deeds. On the one occasion when the Puritan party attempted to translate the paper settlement into reality, the hostile reaction of the government was all too apparent. Nor is there reasonable ground, during this period, for distinguishing between the policy of Hyde and that of the Laudian clergy. No evidence exists of divergence between the political and religious leaders of the Royalist party—to all appearances Hyde and Sheldon were in full accord. . . .

The second stage of the church settlement presents several points of contrast with the first. During the early months of the Restoration, Anglican energies were absorbed in disputing control of the Establishment with the Presbyterian party, initially in possession of the field. So long as the issue was in doubt, we have seen that the Church party had no mind for compromise; the 'rights' of the Church were at stake, and in Laudian eyes, these were not subject to discussion. But by May, 1661, the victory was complete, and with the collapse of Puritanism as a political force, the Presbyterians had ceased even to be dangerous rivals. The nature of the religious problem was thus radically altered. The question was no longer, what compromise would the Presbyterians accept? but what terms would the Anglicans grant? The certainty of Parliamentary support gave the Laudian leaders a sense of freedom in formulating these terms, and it is worth noting that the requirement of episcopal ordination was not a major issue between them and the moderate Puritan group. The subject was not dealt with in the King's Declaration on Ecclesiastical Affairs, which Baxter deemed a sufficient basis for agreement, nor was it a bone of contention in the later discussions. Possibly because many of the Puritan divines were already in episcopal orders, their difficulties were of another sort.

We have shown evidence for believing that the bishops did not enter upon the Savoy Conference in a wholly intransigent frame of mind, and hoped that minor concessions in matters of liturgy and ceremonial might satisfy the opposite party. Under the influence of Baxter, the Presbyterians resolved to present their demands without abatement, and any chance of reconciliation between the two groups disappeared in an outburst of mutual recrimination. Nevertheless, the bishops did not write off all hope of appeasement. From the Laudian standpoint, the revision of the Prayer Book the following autumn was on extremely conservative lines, and showed unmistakable marks of deference to Puritan prejudice. The more temperate attitude of the bishops in this second period is further illustrated by the fact that after May, 1661, the real impetus in the drive against nonconformity passed from the episcopal bench to the House of Commons.

For it was now that the force of Royalist and Anglican reaction in the country at large became the controlling factor in the religious situation. Whereas, in the initial stage, the course of events had been patently directed from above in a calculated and careful strategy, the government found it increasingly difficult to control the rank and file of its supporters. The belligerent Anglicanism of the House of Commons not only showed itself in the degradation of the Covenant and the imposition of a sacramental test on its members. More serious was the fact that it hastily drafted a Bill of Uniformity before the ministry was ready for it, and further embarrassed the government by demanding an arbitrary reversal of the Bill for Settling Ministers passed in the Convention Parliament. These onslaughts against the Puritans were checked, perhaps rather on the ground that they were premature than that they were excessive. But the pressure from below could no longer be contained, and the gradual progress of the Act of Uniformity through Parliament in the spring of 1662 is marked by the increasing severity of its clauses.

Though there are some signs that the bishops favoured a less rigorous policy, the very slightness of the evidence suggests that they gave no strong lead in either direction. But once the Act was approved by King and Parliament, Church leaders took their stand as formerly on the law of the land, and firmly opposed all tampering with its provisions by arbitrary Royal dispensations. It is no less certain that diocesans laboured to retain the vanquished Puritans within the Church. If the terms of peace were high, it is still true that the Laudians preferred a peace that would include the Puritans in their midst to a victory that would drive them from the Church. . . .

Historically, of course, it is impossible to separate the Act of Uniformity from the vindictive legislation enacted soon after against the Puritans by the same Parliament, and supported by many of the bishops. The church settlement of 1662 will always share the stigma which attaches to the so-called 'Clarendon Code'. But since the issues of comprehension and toleration are in essence quite distinct, and since action on the one has endured permanently, while legislation on the other lasted in its full severity less than thirty years, we are justified in considering the Act of Uniformity on its own merits. Historians as a whole have passed a harsh judgment on the Laudian unwillingness to widen the limits of comprehensiveness along the lines of the Royal Declaration, or to accept Puritan demands at the Savoy Conference. Many within the Church of England to-day would agree that an opportunity was tragically lost of retaining the more moderate dissenters in the national Church, and that the sacrifice was made for an ideal of little value. The final refusal in 1662 to come to terms with the Continental Reformation was in this view a major blunder, and productive of many future ills.

Another judgment is possible, however, and is perhaps most forcibly stated by writers who would regard the Laudian position with some detachment. A modern Congregationalist scholar, for example, has remarked:

That the Puritan outlook was a limited one; that its comprehension within the Church, on the terms its representatives proposed, was only possible by a sacrifice of the wider comprehension of Protestant and Catholic attempted in the Anglican compromise; that the bishops had an arguable case in refusing to countenance what they regarded as a radical change in the character of the Church—considerations of this wider and more impartial character did not come within [Calamy's] purview; it was hardly to be expected that they should.[1]

Similar reservations are expressed by a recent secular historian:

> Had the prelates been willing to make a few concessions, it is said, the grim ejections of 1662 need never have taken place. It is a debatable point. The changes which the Puritans wished to make in the Liturgy would have opened the door to the introduction of a most uncompromising Calvinism, in which the variety of opinion and interpretation allowed under the old Prayer Book would have disappeared.... By rejecting such demands, the [Savoy] Conference at least preserved the catholic character of the Church.[2]

Such reflections suggest at least that the matter is not so simply stated as Professor Clark would have us believe: 'Against the hardening bigotry of the Anglicans he [Baxter] could do nothing.'[3] The Laudians firmly rejected the scheme of comprehension offered by a section of the Puritans; they did not decry the ideal of comprehensiveness. On the contrary, they believed and constantly asserted that within traditional Anglican limits a wider range of belief and practice was possible than in any other religious settlement, and later history has not disproved their claim. Because of their stand, the Church of England, alone among post-Reformation bodies, remained constant in its refusal to commit itself to a rigid system of doctrine and practice, and preserved that tension of authority and freedom, of variety and order, which is its unique heritage in the Christian world.

[1] A.G. Matthews, *Calamy Revised*, Oxford University Press, 1934, Introduction, p. xix.

[2] E.W. Kirby in 'The Reconcilers and the Restoration, 1660–1662', *Essays in Modern English History*, Harvard University Press, 1941, 74. For a similar view, cf. D. Ogg, *England in the Reign of Charles II*, Oxford University Press, 1934, I, p. 199.

[3] G.N. Clark, *The Later Stuarts, 1660–1714*, Oxford University Press, 1947 edn, p. 19.

The ecclesiastical settlement which thus took effect has been rightly regarded as a major landmark in English church history, and remains as a permanent achievement of the Laudian party. The Church of England would continue to be the meeting-place of diverse traditions, but, broadly speaking, its essential position and the limits of its comprehensiveness were finally established by the decision made in 1662. If a century before Anglicans had solemnly affirmed that 'the Church of Rome hath erred', the Laudian triumph resulted in a judgment of equal moment—that the *Ecclesia Anglicana* was of another spirit than Geneva. In the Elizabethan settlement the Reformation had been given a peculiarly English expression, and we may interpret the settlement of 1662 as an equally characteristic version of the counter-Reformation.

The Making of the Restoration Settlement, 1649–1662, Dacre Press, Westminster, 1957, pp. xiii–xiv, 278–80, 89, 216–18, 273–7, 282.

24 Anne Whiteman, 1962

The net result of all the talk and pamphlet controversy and high level negotiation was that so far as the ecclesiastical settlement was concerned, as in other matters, Charles II came back without conditions. Probably no effective conditions could have been laid down; perhaps it was better that none should have been attempted. But with the King's return came a change of incalculable importance. The balance of power within the Church in England altered, almost overnight. For the life of the Church had to go on, and this necessitated a thousand decisions, almost all of them now settled in accordance with the wishes of the Anglican sympathizers who came back as the royal advisers. Had a synod to decide the future of the Church been held before the King returned, the Puritans would have been the party in possession; henceforth, and quickly, it became the Anglicans who held the position of advantage.

At this point it may be useful to recall the main problems confronting all, both clergy and laity, who sought to settle the Church in England... Of the points in dispute, some were old controversies, some the result of recent events. In the first place there was the question of the form of church government to be adopted:

was this to be the traditional episcopacy, modified episcopacy, or some kind of Presbyterianism? And what was to be the fate of those who felt unable to conform to it? Secondly, there was the problem of liturgy: should the use of a specified liturgy be legally required, and if so, what form should it take? Thirdly, debate arose about the kind and degree of ceremonial to be enforced. The fourth and fifth problems both arose directly out of what had happened in the Interregnum. It had to be decided how far, on the one hand, non-episcopal ordinations and, on the other, appointments authorized during the last fifteen or twenty years, were valid; the first involved complex theological issues, the second, conflicting claims to the same preferment of men ejected from their livings and men who had since faithfully served the parishes in their stead. Another problem directly arising from recent events was what attitude should be adopted towards those who had taken the Covenant. Lastly, there was the difficulty of determining how the settlement should be made, at what point debate should give place to decisions, and how these decisions should be enforced. For none of these problems was there an easy or universally popular solution, and it is not surprising that the final arrangements left behind them a trail of frustration and disappointment....

Among those responsible for making the settlement Charles II and his adviser Edward Hyde (from 1658 Lord Chancellor, Earl of Clarendon from 1661) were inevitably in the forefront of the negotiations. It is not easy to elucidate the policy of either man. Probably the truth about the date of Charles II's conversion to Rome will never be exactly known; but his preferences and prejudices in religion are at least clear. By temperament strongly attracted to Roman Catholicism, he accepted the political necessity of supporting the Church of England; Anglicanism was not, in his eyes, as suitable a religion for kings as Roman Catholicism, but it was not, like Presbyterianism, unfit for gentlemen. Moreover, Anglicans had for long made loyalty to the monarchy almost another article of the Creed, while Presbyterians had needed political defeat to spur them into a proper allegiance, and even then had forced the King to accept the Covenant as a condition of their help. From Charles's point of view the most satisfactory form of settlement was almost certainly a re-established Church of England, accompanied by toleration for both Roman Catholics and Dissenters, for such would ensure the greatest measure of political support for his régime, and perhaps prepare the way for an eventual conversion of the whole country to Roman Catholicism. For such a policy, hinted at in the Declaration of Breda and explicit in the 1672 Indulgence, he strove long and unsuccessfully against opposition that might well have daunted many men; even with his tempered action, no ecclesiastical group really trusted him.

Clarendon's ecclesiastical standpoint has for long been the subject of intermittent debate. But though in his *Life* he stressed the continuity of his policy and its essentially Anglican character, from 1642 to at least 1663 he appears at times to have been prepared to work for some degree of limited comprehension or toleration alongside the established Church; his bitter reflection that 'it is an unhappy policy, and always unhappily applied, to imagine that that classis of men can be recovered and reconciled by partial concessions, or granting less than they demand', is probably his epitaph on such attempts to find agreement with the Puritans.[1] Dr B.H.G. Wormald's penetrating study of his religious ideas, so much influenced by the Great Tew circle and in some respects so much the same even in the 1670s, shows how he was exposed to the Latitudinarian opinions which characterized some of the group, and, deriving from them a conviction that the essentials of Christianity were simple and few, was probably by no means averse to compromise over things indifferent. What he feared, Wormald argued, were the political consequences of tampering with the established order in the Church; when political stability was the primary objective, as at the Restoration, ecclesiastical change should not be resisted if it seemed desirable.[2] . . .

By the close of 1660 it must have seemed likely to all observers that the Church would be re-established in the old form. . . But there was still hope that some at least of the points at issue might be settled by compromise, and to this end invitations were sent out to both Anglicans and Presbyterians on 25 March 1661 to attend further discussions at what was to be known as the Savoy Conference. It has been argued that the unexpected—and, to the Govern-

---

[1] Edward, Earl of Clarendon, *Life,* Oxford, 1857, 1, p. 546.
[2] B.H.G. Wormald, *Clarendon,* 240 foll., 280 ff, pp. 304–14; for evidence that Clarendon retained, even in his second exile, much the same ideas as earlier, 261 foll.

ment, highly alarming—election of four Presbyterian members
for the City in the new Parliament, and a real though probably
unfounded fear of Presbyterian plots, lay behind this move, an
attempt to show that the ultimate settlement of the Church was
still an open question. It is also maintained that the resounding
Royalist and Anglican triumphs at the polls in the rest of the
country so renewed the Government's confidence in the soundness
of their position that they were emboldened on 10 April to issue
writs for a Convocation which, after some months of restored
episcopal discipline in the dioceses, might be expected to consist
of proctors solidly for the continuation of the *status quo* in the
Church. Certainly, as in the case of Parliament as a whole, the
elections were completely satisfactory from the Anglican point
of view. But the fact that at first Convocation's terms of reference
were strictly limited suggests that the Savoy Conference was to
be given a real chance to produce something constructive. The
Government's action in preventing a premature Bill for uniformity,
originating in the fanatically Anglican House of Commons, from
proceeding through the Lords, may also have sprung from this
desire to see if a compromise settlement were possible.

But unfortunately hopes that the Savoy Conference would
result in an agreement between Anglicans and Puritans were
doomed to failure....

It would be difficult to find a sadder example of misapplied zeal
than Baxter's determination to strive with the Anglicans almost
single-handed in these discussions. Not only were his tactics
misconceived; he was also already on such uneasy terms with the
Anglican leaders—particularly Morley—that his criticisms and
suggestions were unlikely to get a ready welcome. A man with a
more flexible political sense must have grasped that whatever wide
concessions might have been hoped for at an earlier stage in the
negotiations, Anglican fortunes had now risen so decisively that
there was no longer any question of attaining the Puritan ideal;
it was merely a matter of what could be salvaged from the wreck
of their hopes. Baxter records that he moderated the criticisms
and requests put forward; but a perusal of the papers the Puritans
produced gives the impression that they did not find it possible
to distinguish between matters which to those without a Puritan
conscience seemed of minor importance, and matters of generally
acknowledged significance. Baxter's burning sincerity and in-

defatigable spirit, merits though they were, were less useful to the Puritans at this juncture than political suavity and *finesse* could have been; but these were qualities utterly despised by the Puritan negotiators of this generation, and it is a measure of their integrity as men that this was so.

...The Act of Uniformity finally passed both Houses after a conference on 30 April, and received the royal assent on 19 May, without any provision for mitigating its requirements. If it had been Clarendon's aim, as seems possible, to avoid a rigid, unaccommodating settlement, he had not succeeded.

The revised Prayer Book and the Act of Uniformity together set out the conditions for conformity to the Church of England, and settled the fate of Puritan incumbents who, by 24 August 1662, had to decide whether they could with a good conscience stay in the Church, or must suffer deprivation...It was the bitter fate of the Puritans not only to lose their preferments but to feel that nothing of all they had fought for so single-mindedly would come to fruition within the framework of a national comprehensive Church, in which most of them believed as firmly as their Anglican opponents. Men like Calamy and Baxter, Manton and Bates had no desire to found a sect, and only the witness they felt they must make, and their responsibility to their congregations, led them to carry on their ministry outside the Church. Some, like John Ray and Zachary Crofton, resigned their preferments and became conforming members, but as if they had been laymen, of the Church of England.

The conditions demanded by the Act of Uniformity were, then, admittedly not easy; they required more than had ever been asked for before from ministers in the Church of England, and asked for it with a new precision particularly hard on men with minds so scrupulous that the exact wording of every phrase and the exact meaning of every word had to be examined with meticulous and personal care, as the discussions over the demand for 'consent' and 'assent' to the contents of the Prayer Book showed. The revisers of the liturgy, it is true, had paid some respect to Puritan wishes expressed in the talks of 1661, and the result was a disappointment to some High Churchmen who would have liked something more akin to the 1549 text, but the final version was still full of things in which Puritans could not acquiesce. When it became clear that the non-subscribers would be many, the politicians seem to have been more concerned than the Anglican clergy themselves. Clarendon's speech at the adjournment on 19 May reaffirmed his desire for eventual comprehension; throughout the summer there was talk of a toleration or an indulgence. The Lord Chancellor made two attempts to mitigate the effects of the Act: the first in June, when he tried unsuccessfully to get a general suspension of it; the second in August, when the opposition of Sheldon prevented a scheme by which individual dispensations might have been granted by the King. But the Anglicans who opposed any suspension or indulgence also had a reputable point of view. They had also fought hard for the re-establishment of what they considered to be the essentials of their Church: episcopal government, a standard liturgy, adherence to a minimum of ceremonial. Some, like Thorndike, felt that it was their prime duty to retain what they had in common with the communion of the Catholic Church, and saw the problem of unity in different terms. Within limits they had been prepared to make concessions to Puritan scruples, certainly once they had won their main position, perhaps even before. But on other points they could compromise no more than the Puritans, so that the area in which agreement was possible was from the first small.

In the skirmishing that accompanied the re-establishment of the Church of England between 1660 and 1662, neither side has an entirely creditable record. Because they were ultimately the losers, and because the results of their defeat were so tragic for themselves and for the unity of the Church, the Puritans command a sympathy which, perhaps, they do not in all respects deserve. It is easy to see them as the helpless victims of a powerful and vengeful Royalist and Anglican machine, which remorselessly drove them to their doom. But in the Convention Parliament their party played their political cards as ruthlessly as did the Anglicans after the next election, and with as little regard for the injustice they might do to individuals who also had a case worth arguing. They were certainly unfortunate in that no clerical leader with first-rate political capacity emerged from their ranks, and they were poorly supported by their lay friends who, bought off with honours and office, left the ministers to fight virtually alone. Yet when all that is said, it is difficult to acquit the Puritans of a certain blindness in their conduct of affairs: an unwillingness to see that Presbyterians and Independents had to stand together; a fundamental inability to distinguish between essentials and superficialities which weakened the respect their opponents were prepared to pay to their scruples, and a political obtuseness as to what, at any time, was a feasible rather than an ideal policy. Good men though their leaders were, and good as was much in their cause, they were often too ready to attribute honest disagreement with their own point of view to mere obstinacy or even deliberate malice; they were dangerously sure that they alone had right on their side. '...We spoke to the Deaf', wrote Baxter of the failure of the Savoy Conference; but deafness was not the infirmity of one side only. Both Anglicans and Puritans, in the prolonged controversies, had difficulty in hearing the voice of charity and the arguments of reason.

The Anglicans from the start had many advantages: the support of the King for at any rate much of their programme, zealous lay co-operation, the legal argument that they were the legitimate heirs kept from their heritage by wicked usurpers. Much in the political situation, after the first few months, was overwhelmingly in their favour, and they knew how to exploit it, deliberately, and, at times, somewhat unscrupulously. They could afford to offer concessions, but how far they were ever ready to compromise with the Puritans except on a superficial level remains uncertain; undeniably, if we knew more of the mind of Charles II, Clarendon, Morley, and Sheldon, the chief architects of the settlement, we could better judge the sincerity with which the negotiations were carried out. None of them, it appears, was wholly averse to some degree of accommodation; even Sheldon voted for the unsuccessful proviso to allow the King to dispense with the requirements of the Act of Uniformity in favour of individual ministers. But of the four men, his aims were perhaps the simplest: to restore the Church of England to its traditional form, with as few changes as possible, and, once this had been achieved, to refuse any further negotiations. Yet with all his strength, courage, and decision, he could, it seems, be strangely blind to the implications of his actions, or of what he acquiesced in. The prominence of Parliament and comparative inconspicuousness of Convocation in the making of the 1662 settlement further weakened the Church in its relations with the State, while his short-sighted agreement of 1664 with Clarendon over the taxation of the clergy, which led almost immediately to the virtual suspension of Convocation, deprived the Church of its official mouthpiece and stripped it of its last shred of independence. Perhaps some similar defect of vision played a part in his making of the 1662 settlement; perhaps he did not really believe that the intensely individual Puritans, with whom he had to deal, could ever become the founders of the permanent force in English life which Dissent turned out to be. Odd remarks that he is said, on not very good authority, to have made at this time, are often quoted to support the view that he did not regret the removal of the Puritans from the Church, and this may be true. But it seems more likely that he thought that the judicious use of force would soon restore uniformity, and counted the temporary suffering cheap if a really united and disciplined Church could thereby soon be achieved. Such a view now wins no sympathy, but it was still a common attitude in Europe in the middle of the seventeenth century, and sincerely held by Churchmen of more obvious spirituality than Sheldon.

From Uniformity to Unity, 1662–1962, ed. G.F. Nuttall and Owen Chadwick, S.P.C.K., 1962, pp. 52–5, 75–8, 81–6.

Local Solutions

25 Richard Baxter, 1696

[At the Savoy conference, the bishops] told me that it was we that had filled the people's heads with these scruples, and then, when we should dispossess them of them, we pleaded for their liberty: if I would but teach the people better, they would quickly be brought to obedience, and would need no liberty. I told the bishop that he was much mistaken, both in saying that we put these scruples into their heads, and in thinking that my power with them was so great, as that I alone could preach them out. He replied with great confidence that if I would but endeavour in good earnest to satisfy them, they would quickly be satisfied. . . . And I many times told him and the rest that I perceived that it was like to be a great wrong to us, and a greater to themselves and the kingdom, that they mistakingly imagined our power to be greater with the people than it is, and that they think we could reduce them at our pleasure to conformity, when it is no such matter; and that they imagine that the godly people who dissent from them do pin their religion so absolutely on our sleeves and take up all their opinions on trust from us. Whereas I assured him that he will find by experience that so many of them know why they hold what they hold, and do it so purely for conscience sake, that if all we should turn and set against them, there would so many thousands continue in their opinions as I would not be a persecutor of, or excommunicate, for more than ever their Lordships will get by it. . . .

To return to Bishop Morley: he told me when he silenced me that he would take care that the people should be no losers, but should be taught as well as they were by me. And when I was gone, he got awhile a few scandalous men, with some that were more civil, to keep up the lecture, till the paucity of their auditors gave them a pretence to put it down. And he came himself one day and preached to them a long invective against them and me, as Presbyterians, and I know not what, so that the people wondered that ever a man would venture to come up into a pulpit and speak so confidently to a people that he knew not, the things which they commonly knew to be untrue. And this sermon was so far from winning any of them to the estimation of their new bishop or curing that which he called the admiration of my person (which was his great endeavour) that they were much confirmed in their former judgments. But still the bishop looked at Kidderminster as a factious, schismatical, Presbyterian people, that must be cured of their overvaluing of me, and then they would be cured of all the rest; whereas if he had lived with them the twentieth part so long as I had done, he would have known that they were neither Presbyterians, nor factious, nor schismatical, nor seditious, but a people that quietly followed their hard labour, and learned the Holy Scriptures, and lived a holy, blameless life in humility and peace with all men, and never had any sect or separated party among them, but abhorred all faction and sidings in religion, and lived in love and Christian unity.

Matthew Sylvester, *Reliquiae Baxterianae*, 1696, pp. 345, 375–6.

26 The Bishop of Exeter, 1663

Letter to Archbishop Sheldon, 19 December 1663

My diocese had not one outed presbyter who dared to preach publicly for these twelve months past (at least which I have heard of), till a while since one Quick, ejected out of Brixton, undertook boldly to preach there. I did what I was obliged to do, and he is now prisoner (and so in a fair way to become rich) in the Castle of Exon, to which he was brought this week. He saith that after his removal he stayed some months to see whether any other would supply his place, but at length finding that no man was put in his stead and that the people went off, some to atheism and

debauchery, others to sectarism (for he is a Presbyterian) he resolved to adventure to gather his flock again. And he had gathered,
as I am told, a flock of 1,500 or 2,000 upon Sunday last when by
the warrant of Sir Tho. Hele and Sir Wm. Strode he was taken
from the pulpit and brought away.

A.G. Matthews, *Calamy Revised,* Oxford University Press, 1934,
p. 402.

27   Sir Peter Leicester, 1677

*Spoken in his Charge to the Grand Jury at Nether
Knutsford, Cheshire, 2 October, 1677*

Our old implacable enemies the Papists, with all their new
enchanted crew of sectaries of all sorts...every justice of peace in
his station must make it his business strictly to find them out; for
the country people are generally so rotten that they will not
complain of them, though they see and know of these seditious
meetings before their eyes daily.

*Charges to the Grand Jury at Quarter Sessions, 1660–1677 by Sir Peter
Leicester,* ed. E.M. Halcrow, Chetham Society, 3rd ser., v, 1953,
p. 91.

Local Solutions in Perspective

28   Robert S. Bosher, 1957

Re-establishment of the old system proceeded steadily at the parish level.... The seventeenth-century Justices of the Peace were officials managing all the details of local government, recruited from the local gentry, and possessed of wide powers. Since their appointment was in the hands of the Crown, many Cavalier squires like Isham had been quickly placed in office during the early months of the Restoration by a government desperately anxious to secure firm control of the country at large.... On all sides, complaints of arbitrary action and minor persecution were heard from sorely harassed Puritan ministers.... Royalist magistrates were not inclined to take their tone from the studied moderation of the Court, with its promises of toleration and concession....

This ruthless determination to enforce the old Church laws without further delay was to be seen on all sides.... Beginning in September, prosecutions were undertaken against ministers in many parts of the country who refused to read the Prayer Book. Mr A.G. Matthews notes cases tried during the autumn months, both in the Assizes and Quarter Sessions, in counties as widely scattered as Shropshire, Sussex, Staffordshire, Nottinghamshire, Cheshire, Middlesex, Devon, and Northumberland.[1]...

The indulgence granted in these matters by the King's Declaration of October 25 seems hardly to have dampened the churchly zeal of the Justices.

The Making of the Restoration Settlement, 1649–1662, Westminster, Dacre Press, 1957, pp. 199–202.

[1] A.G. Matthews, *Calamy Revised*, I, pp. 42, 143, 193, 203, 221, 315, 420.

29   Christopher Hill, 1967

Class lines were drawn tighter after 1660. Dissenters 'are not excluded from the nobility', wrote John Corbet in 1667; 'among the gentry they are not a few, but none are of more importance than they in the trading part of the people, and those that live by industry, upon whose hands the business of the nation lies much.' They tended to trade perforce with one another, and this accentuated the split between nonconformist town and Anglican countryside.

Between 1662 and 1689 persecution was intermittent but often severe. Long periods in gaol, arbitrary fines, the general insecurity and sometimes sheer plunder of their goods ruined many of the small craftsmen from whom nonconformity's strength was drawn. On the other hand the exclusion of dissenters from state office and universities drove them into business. Much of the moral energy which had been devoted to politics was now turned to more material ends. The Lancashire textile trades appear to have been built up in the seventeenth and early eighteenth centuries by dissenters. Celia Fiennes in her tour of 1695–7 frequently noted the connection between nonconformity and enclosure. That nonconformity led to business success was a commonplace by the end of the century. The Quakers indeed had reason to bewail the decline in religious zeal as members of their community prospered. Many before Wesley noted the disturbing cycle, that godliness led to hard work which led to wealth which led to ungodliness. English industry also benefited from the immigration of thousands of Huguenot craftsmen, especially silk-weavers, notably after Louis xiv's Revocation of the Edict of Nantes in 1685. Economic writers began to advocate liberty of conscience precisely because it would attract foreign immigrants and discourage emigration, as well as because of the economic importance of dissenters.

Christopher Hill, *Reformation to Industrial Revolution: a social and economic history of Britain, 1530–1780,* Weidenfeld and Nicolson, 1967, pp. 155–6.

30   G.M. Trevelyan, 1944

After the Restoration, the members of the landowning class who attended conventicles and suffered persecution as Nonconformists were a mere handful. Anglicanism became distinctively the upper class religion, far more completely than it had been in the days of Elizabeth or of Laud. There were indeed still a certain number of Roman Catholic country-gentlemen, especially in Lancashire and Northumberland; they were shut out from all participation in local and national government by laws which the King was occasionally able to break for their benefit. Otherwise the upper class, the gentlemen of England, were socially united by common conformity to the Anglican worship. Henceforth the services of the parish church were under the special patronage of the ladies and gentlemen in the family pew; the great body of the congregation were their dependents, the farmers and labourers of the village. Addison's Sir Roger de Coverley in church affords a pleasant example of the social side of rural worship as it remained for many generations to come:

> My friend Sir Roger, being a good Church-man, has beautified the inside of his Church with several texts of his own choosing. He has likewise given a handsome pulpit cloth and railed in the communion table at his own expense. He has often told me that at his coming to his estate he found the Parishioners very irregular; and in order to make them kneel and join in the responses, he gave every one of them a hassock and a Common-Prayer book; and at the same time employed an itinerant singing-master, who goes about the country for that purpose, to instruct them rightly in the tunes of the Psalms. As Sir Roger is landlord to the whole congregation, he keeps them in very good order, and suffers nobody to sleep in it besides himself; for if by chance he has been surprised into a short nap at sermon, upon recovering out of it he stands up and looks about him, and if he sees anybody else nodding, either wakes them himself or sends his servants to them.

The dissenting congregations, on the other hand, alike in times of persecution and toleration, were made up of men who prided themselves on their independence, and who liked to feel that the chapel and its minister belonged to themselves. Socially at least they were 'at ease in Zion,' safe from the inquisitorial eye of the squire and his lady. Until the Wesleyan movement, dissenting congregations and meetings were almost confined to cities, market towns and industrial districts, though many villages had isolated families of Quakers and Baptists. Some of the Dissenters were poor artisans like John Bunyan; others, especially in London and Bristol, were wealthy merchants who could have bought up the squires who persecuted them. And often such merchants did in fact buy out needy gentlemen, after accumulating mortgages on their land. In the next generation the dissenting merchant's son would be a squire and a churchman. Yet another generation, and the ladies of the family would be talking with contempt of all who attended meeting-houses or engaged in trade!

Thus the social character of English religious divisions was stereotyped at the Restoration and continued with little change until the Victorian era. . . .

For a generation after 1660 the Puritans were often bitterly persecuted, but more for political and social reasons than from genuinely religious motives. The object of the 'Clarendon Code' was to prevent the revival of the Roundhead party, and to avenge the wrongs suffered by Anglicans and Cavaliers. But the spirit of the persecution was not ecclesiastical; it was not a heresy hunt. The hard-drinking foxhunters of the manor-house hated the Presbyterians of the neighbouring Town not because they held the doctrines of Calvin, but because they talked through their noses, quoted scripture instead of swearing honest oaths, and voted Whig instead of Tory.

English Social History. A Survey of Six Centuries, Chaucer to Victoria,
Longmans, 1944, pp. 253–6.

31 G.M. Trevelyan, 1926

The religious settlement of the Restoration was not conceived in the spirit of compromise which marked the political and social settlement. Yet it may at least be questioned whether it has not led to more religious, intellectual and political liberty than would have resulted from a wider extension of the boundaries of the Established Church. If the plan to 'comprehend' Baxter and the moderate Puritans had succeeded at the abortive Savoy Conference of 1661, the Quakers, Baptists, and more advanced sects, who must still have been left outside, might have been too isolated and inconsiderable ever to enforce the claim of toleration for themselves. The arrangement actually made, under which the Church of England and the various Puritan Churches followed each its own lines of development, rendered toleration inevitable ere long, and led to the variety and competition of religious bodies characteristic of modern England, utterly at variance with mediæval, Tudor or Stuart notions of Church and State.

It is true that the Puritan sects lost greatly by exclusion from the culture of the Universities and from their natural share in social influence and political power, but their very disabilities and grievances forced them to remain for two hundred years vigilant champions of liberty and critics of government. Our two-party system in politics flourished so long and so vigorously because religion also was based upon the two great parties of privileged and unprivileged. . . .

It is, indeed, remarkable how much of Puritan, or at least of strongly Protestant thought and practice survived the political and ecclesiastical fall of the Puritan sects. Family prayer and Bible reading had become national custom among the great majority of religious laymen, whether they were Churchmen or Dissenters. The English character had received an impression from Puritanism which it bore for the next two centuries, though it had rejected Puritan coercion and had driven Dissenters out of polite society. Even the Puritan Sunday survived. The anxiety of James I and Laud that the English people should continue as of old to play

74

games on Sunday afternoon, was, one would have supposed, calculated to meet with the approval of the most athletic and 'sporting' of all nations. Yet even at the Restoration, when the very name of Puritan was a hissing and a reproach, when the gaols were crowded with harmless Quakers and Baptists, the Puritan idea of Sunday, as a day strictly set aside for rest and religious meditation, continued to hold the allegiance of the English people. The good and evil effects of this self-imposed discipline of a whole nation, in abstaining from organized amusement as well as from work on every seventh day, still awaits the dispassionate study of the social historian.

History of England (1926) Longmans, 1952 edn, pp. 450–1, 453.

32   William Haller, 1960

It may well be that it was this fixing of the cleavage of English life at the centre into church and nonconformity which was the Restoration's most significant contribution to the development of the English-speaking community at large.

. . . Religion was made, not the bond of union among the English people as they presently swarmed out into the world, but more than ever an arena for the free play of all sorts of differences of class, education, social aspiration, nationality, and political interest, as well as of simple religious conviction. In one way and another, religion continued to be a threat, though a diminishing one, to the stability of the civil order itself. . . . For what both Elizabeth and the second Charles were up against was a revolution of an unprecedented kind, a kind which our own age is in a better position to appreciate, a profound cultural revolution set off by a technological invention directly affecting the mental lives and habits of all members of society and sooner or later the structure and functioning of every institution. The invention of printing and the development of the book trade in its multifarious branches evoked an abounding vernacular literature, using that term in its broadest sense, and with it an articulate vernacular public which might never agree as to exactly what it wanted but always knew that it had wants for government to satisfy. The development of such a public confronted rulers, supposedly ruling by Divine Right, with the infinitely complicated and perplexing problem of exercising that right in the face of an extremely active, vociferous, and pervasive public opinion swayed this way and that by all the winds of doctrine, gusts of personal and party interest, and aspirations of nationality that blew. The success of rulers in maintaining the position which in theory they owed only to God depended in fact on the degree of their ability to ride the storm which, thanks to the printing press, religion more than anything else had stirred up in men's minds.

The Restoration of the Stuarts, Blessing or Disaster?, Report of a Folger Library Conference, 1960, Folger Shakespeare Library, Washington, pp. 43–5.

33   Douglas Lacey, 1969

The gradations of dissent

There was too wide a variety and too great an intensity of religious belief prevalent in England at the Restoration for Anglican leaders to realize their hopes of attaining religious uniformity. Instead, the new Act of Uniformity and the first Conventicle Act completed the transformation of Puritanism into Dissent. And just as there previously had been a great diversity of belief and practice among Puritans, likewise many gradations of Dissent appeared among those who refused to conform completely to the restored Anglican Church. As a result, even though the new laws seemed to have created a great gulf between those who conformed and those who did not, the distinctions between Anglicans and Dissenters were frequently so fine that it has always been difficult to establish the distinguishing characteristics of Dissent and to lay down a realistic line of demarcation.

After decades of hoping to reform or change the Established Church to suit their views, devout and moderate Puritans could not suddenly accept the very ceremonies, practices, and hierarchy they had sought to eliminate or modify. Consequently they felt compelled to become Dissenters along with the more extreme Puritans who were Sectarian, Separatist, or Independent in tradition. Yet unlike these Puritans who had always wanted to remain outside the Anglican Church and enjoy toleration, this was not the status the moderate Puritans had wanted. Their attitude did not change when they became Dissenters. In their dissent they therefore did not become complete Nonconformists. Instead they adopted the practice of occasional or partial conformity. Very shortly after the Restoration, therefore, terms such as 'conformable Nonconformist' came into existence to describe those who conformed in varying degrees. But the most revealing description of this sector of the religious spectrum lying between uncompromising Dissent and complete Anglicanism was the title of a work written later by John Cheyney—*The Conforming Non-conformist and the Non-conforming Conformist.* 'The title of my book is the image of my mind,' wrote Cheyney, and there were many others who could have said the same.

Dissent and Parliamentary Politics in England, 1661–1689, Rutgers University Press, 1969, pp. 15–16.

34   Anne Whiteman, 1955

By 1663 episcopal administration was in full working order and the re-establishment of the church a reality in most parishes throughout the land. Only gradually did it become apparent that, so far as Parliament and Convocation were concerned, the old system was to be restored unaltered except for the abolition of High Commission and the proscription of the *ex officio* oath....

In view of the attacks on the traditional organization which had preceded the Civil War, this omission to carry through any reforms of its less efficient or less popular aspects itself deserves attention. It must be asked how true it is to say that a unique opportunity for reform did exist in these years, and also how serious, both from a short-term and a long-term point of view, was the failure to modify the traditional system. As events were to turn out, conditions in the next hundred and fifty years were scarcely favourable to the implementation of the many plans for its improvement. Convocation was more or less shelved, Parliament was to find concern with political rather than administrative questions, and it was left to nineteenth-century legislation effectually to modify the basic medieval organization. . . .

Nowhere is the basic conservatism of the re-establishment of the church better seen than in the revival of its judicial authority. Except for High Commission, the numerous Courts of the ordinary and peculiar jurisdictions took up again unaltered the powers they had exercised before the Civil War, save for the *ex officio* oath. Moral cases as well as those arising from breaches of ecclesiastical discipline still came before them, and they had jurisdiction also in matrimonial and testamentary matters, in defamation and in many cases involving tithe. Procedure remained cumbrous and slow and cases often dragged on for over a year. Fees obviously varied, but at Exeter those who appeared once only and satisfied the court often had to pay as much as 5s or 6s 4d. Compurgation was still used, and so was public penance. . . . Particularly resented was the use of excommunication to enforce obedience to court orders. The inevitable result is clear in the comment of a Wiltshire-man that 'he cared not for the Court nor power of it, it was but Excommunication'. . . .

The ecclesiastical records of the Restoration show, then, how exactly in almost every way the pre-Civil War administration was revived in the years 1660 to 1663, and how faithfully the Church of England, in all its minor ramifications as well as in the central political sphere, was re-established. In the years following the Restoration the revived system worked in many ways well, and if some aspects of it, such as its inquisitorial powers with regard to morals, were soon to grow anachronistic, they may perhaps be regarded as of a piece with the remnants of paternalism in secular government which survived the Restoration, but were to perish or lose their significance at or soon after the Revolution. So far as the Church was concerned, the administrative system as re-established at the Restoration was to remain structurally unchanged until the nineteenth century, but much of the spirit of conviction which still animated it when it was revived, and made tolerable its shortcomings, was gradually to disappear. In ecclesiastical administration as well as in theology, it was rather the change in mental climate in the last years of the seventeenth century than the cataclysm in the middle of it which divided the Church of Whitgift and Laud from that of Herring and Hoadly.

'The re-establishment of the Church of England, 1660–1663', *Transactions of the Royal Historical Society,* fifth series, v, 1955, pp. 111–13, 117–18, 130–1.

Part Three

THE LAND SETTLEMENT

When the possibility of a restoration of the king was first discussed, the attitude of purchasers of confiscated land, and the policy to be adopted towards them, figured prominently in debate. Some thought they were a large and influential group who must be placated. Others thought they were too few to deserve consideration. Charles II did not underestimate the problem, and directed some cautious but conciliatory words at purchasers in July 1659, offering them recompense for what they might lose by supporting his return (35). A letter allegedly from General Monk in January 1660 to the Devonshire gentry (36) maintained that purchasers of confiscated estates, along with other supporters of Parliament, were too powerful for anyone even to contemplate restoring the monarchy. But at the same time, in February 1660, Lord Chancellor Hyde was dismissing purchasers as an inconsiderable group compared with the nation as a whole, and quite incapable of stemming a rising popular tide in favour of Charles's return. Yet he too offered them the prospect of compensation if they came forward to support the king (37).

A month after the Restoration a pamphleteer prophesied confusion and ruin if purchasers had to restore their lands to their former owners (38). In the event, the terms of the settlement were left to Parliament to decide, and no single piece of legislation dealt with the whole problem at a stroke and on one uniform basis. This explains why subsequent commentators have disagreed about the outcome.

Charles II ordered a careful investigation of all claimants to church lands, including former lessees, Commonwealth purchasers, and sitting tenants, and proposed that new leases be issued in the light of the situation thus revealed, in accordance with justice and equity. His instructions to the Archbishop of Canterbury (39) indicate the spirit in which he intended the settlement of church and crown lands to be carried out. In practice, resentments and recrimination bedevilled negotiations with the Church, and in Clarendon's view the latter earned an ill reputation by its handling of the affair (40). The crown does not seem to have been similarly castigated.

Royalist propagandists made the most of their party's financial difficulties after 1660, and blamed the land settlement as a factor contributing to the impoverishment of the king's friends. Royalist bitterness has tended to colour the general verdict on the land settlement, and, until recently, it was usually argued that Parliament's sales, together with other land sales forced on Royalists by composition fines and other levies, created a new class of upstart landowners who held on to their gains at the Restoration. Edward Waterhouse wrote cynically in this vein in 1665 (41). The Reverend H.E. Chesney, writing in 1932, took the same view (42).

More recent studies on the identity of the purchasers of confiscated land during the Interregnum and on the Restoration settlement have reversed this verdict. Dr Thirsk shows that Parliament gradually felt its way towards the only reasonable settlement of the land problem, namely, a compromise involving concessions on both sides. In restoring Crown and Church lands a compromise was possible. The problem of restoring royalists' land, however was of a different nature (43). H.J. Habakkuk, having investigated other private sales of land by Royalists, judges their long-term effects on the pattern of landownership (44). Land sales during the Civil War and Interregnum cannot be said to have established a new class of landowners.

The effects of the sales on the efficient use of land are illustrated in the Duchess of Newcastle's description of her husband's estates (45), and in Ian Gentles's account of the changes wrought on Crown lands (46). Christopher Hill argues for a fundamental change in agrarian relationships and attitudes as a permanent result of the Interregnum land sales (47).

The Land Settlement in Prospect, 1659-60

35 Charles II, 1659

In a letter to Mr Mordaunt, July, 1659

I know not what to say more to those who are possessed of my lands or the church lands of my friends than that if any will frankly engage in my service and shall perform anything of merit in it, I will make him an equal recompense for what he shall lose by returning to his duty, and this I think will satisfy any man who doth in his heart wish well to me. But if I should make any general offers to that purpose it would discredit me with many good men and make little impression to my advantage with those who are most concerned; men naturally giving little credit to promises which are hardly possible to be performed.

Clarendon State Papers, Oxford, 1767–86, III, pp. 512–13.

36 General Monk, 1660

Letter from General Monk, 23 January 1660, to the Gentlemen of Devonshire

Most Honoured and Dear Friends
...Before these unhappy wars the government of these nations was monarchical in church and state. These wars have given birth and growth to several interests both in church and state heretofore not known, though now upon many accounts very considerable, as the Presbyterian, Independent, Anabaptist, and sectaries of all sorts, as to ecclesiastics, and the purchasers of the King's, Queen's,

Princes', bishops', deans' and chapters' and all other forfeited estates, and all these engaged in these wars against the king as to *civils*. Those interests again are so interwoven by purchases and intermarriages, and thereby forfeited, as I think upon rational grounds it may be taken for granted that no government can be either good, peaceful, or lasting to these nations that doth not rationally include and comprehend the security and preservation of all the aforesaid interests both civil and spiritual, I mean so far as by the word of God they are warranted to be protected and preserved.

If this be so, then that government under which we formerly were, viz. monarchy, cannot possibly be admitted for the future in these nations because its support is taken away, and because it is exclusive of all the former interests both civil and spiritual, all of them being incompatible with monarchical uniformity in church and state thus expired. That government then that is most able to comprehend and protect all interests, as is aforesaid, must needs be republick.

White Kennett, *A Register and Chronicle Ecclesiastical and Civil*, 1728, p. 32.

37 Edward Hyde, later Lord Clarendon, 1660

In a letter to Mr Barwick, 20 February 1660

I do confess to you, though very many are of your opinion, and would find out expedients accordingly, I am not so much frighted with the fear of those persons who, by being possessed of the church, crown, and delinquents' lands, will be thereby withheld from returning to their duty, except they might be assured to retain the same. First, I do not think the number so very considerable of all those who are entangled in that guilt, that their interest can continue or support the war, when the nation shall discern that there is nothing else keeps off the peace. Secondly, they who have the greatest share in these spoils are persons otherwise too irreconcilable either by their guilt as the King's murderers or their villainous resolutions, as Sir Arthur Haslerig and others, that no overtures of that kind would work upon them, but would be turned into reproach; and as the number of those is not great, so the greatness of their possessions makes them more enemies than friends, setting all other guilt aside. Thirdly, as it is not in the King's power to alienate either Crown, Church, or delinquents' lands, therefore, his offer, if he should make it, would be valued accordingly; and it is hardly possible that any Parliament who owns the King can be so constituted as to ratify such an alienation; so no particular man, who is possessed of such lands and will really do as signal service for the King can doubt but that it is in the King's power, and must be in his will, to make him ample recompense for any service he shall do him, and that he shall be a good husband, as well as a good subject, by returning to his duty and serving the King effectually; and therefore, you may safely undertake from the King and in his name to Colonel Redman that he shall not find his fortune the worse for serving the King, but that if he shall do it vigorously he shall be sure either to have a good title given him to the lands in Ireland of which he is possessed, or at least to continue him in the possession of them till he receives a valuable recompense to his own satisfaction.

Clarendon State Papers, Oxford, 1767–86, III, p. 687.

38 Anon, 1660

Of the Weight of Concernees

That the weight of purchasers may be the better known, it were fit to consider severally the first purchasers, other under-purchasers and claimants under them, heirs apparent, expectants of the estate, their kindred and relations. The purchasers are known many of them not to have bought barely for the sake of a purchase but with design of some special disposal of their persons, removing themselves and families from other places and employments to which they cannot return but with unspeakable loss. Where others have bought for the sake of a revenue, it will be found that many of them have disposed their other estates in advancement of their children and now rely upon the new for subsistence, many of them bought reversions that have not yielded them anything more than an old rent of about a twentieth part, the other nineteen parts not yielding a penny. In other cases, the new estates being incorporate with the old, and by wills and settlements put into the walls and foundations of families, the pulling down of such corners and principals will spoil the building. . . .

The underpurchasers are known generally to have paid near as much as the like estates are worth upon the best titles. Some because they were immediate tenants, others because the land lay mixt with their own, but most from the reputation these titles had gotten in common opinion by succession of so many years and the engagement of men of all parties. Many of them bought very lately and have received little or nothing, others paid double the first purchase for improvements and casual advantages fallen to the first buyers by the deaths of tenants for lives.

Derivative claimers under these are multitudes of women entitled to dowers and jointures, others claiming in recompense of other estates by partitions, exchanges, and settlements in marriage, some as trustees and executors for orphans and charitable uses, others for security of debts, by mortgages, statutes, judgments, and recognizances, some again who relied upon the bonds and credit of their debtors, esteemed owners of such lands, but being deprived thereof are disable to pay their debts; to all these may be added tenants who in cities and good towns have paid great fines, altered their old and built new houses, of which there are whole streets about London; other tenants in the country have laid out of all they are worth in building, enclosure, and other improvements. There are manors that have many copyholders for life who have bought in their own lives and entitled their wives to the customary estate, many, both copyholders and others, have surrendered their old estates for life or years to take new or to entitle their sons, all which estates will be avoidable if the sales be avoided, and an inlet made to most vexatious suits upon warranties, covenants of assurance, and other colours both in law and equity to the ruin of all these families and the bringing in of endless confusion.

Some Considerations offered to Publique View in Behalf of the Many Thousand Persons Interessed in Publique Sales; wherein is shortly stated 1. The original of publique debts satisfied upon those sales; 2. the consideration of the sales themselves and their authorities; 3. the consonancy of their confirmation to presidents of law and the practises of former times; 4. the weight of the concernees, London, 3 July 1660, pp. 6–7.

The Land Settlement in Progress

39 Charles II, 1660

*Charless II's letter to the Archbishop of Canterbury,
13 October 1660*

Carolus Rex

Most Reverend Father in God, we greet you well;

Being tender of our engagements to have a care for the reasonable satisfaction of tenants and purchasers of Church lands, our will and pleasure is that you give order to all Bishops, Deans and Chapters within your province that in letting the lands and revenues belonging to their respective churches, they have regard to such as were tenants before the late troubles, where they have not parted with their leases, giving them not only the privilege of pre-emption before any others, but using them with all favour and kindness; and you are forthwith to give such directions that no grant or lease be made of things purchased by any officer or soldier of the army, or others, unless it be the purchaser, or by his consent, until we take further order, which we shall do speedily, it being our intention to be very careful of the church's interest.

Given at our Court at Whitehall, the 13th of October in the twelfth year of our reign.

White Kennett, *A Register and Chronicle Ecclesiastical and Civil*, 1728, p. 279.

40 Lord Clarendon, 1672

They called their old tenants to account for rent, and to renew their estates if they had a mind to it; for most old leases were expired in the long continuance of the war, and the old tenants had been compelled either to purchase a new right and title from the state (when the Ordinance was passed for taking away all Bishops, Deans and Chapters, and for selling all the lands which belonged to them), or to sell their present estates to those, who had purchased the reversion and the inheritance thereof. So that both the one and the other, the old tenants and the new purchasers, repaired to the true owners as soon as the King was restored; the former expecting to be restored again to the possession of what they had sold, under an unreasonable pretence of a tenant right (as they called it), because there remained yet (as in many cases there did) a year or some other term of their old leases unexpired, and because they had out of conscience forborne to buy the inheritance of the church, which was first offered to them. And for the refusal thereof, and such a reasonable fine as was usual, they hoped to have a new lease, and to be readmitted to be tenants to the church. The other, the purchasers (amongst which there were some very infamous persons), appeared as confident, and did not think that, according to the clemency that was practised towards all sorts of men, it could be thought justice, that they should lose the entire sum they had disbursed upon the faith of that government, which the whole kingdom submitted to; but that they should, instead of the inheritance they had an ill title to, have a good lease for lives or years granted to them by them who had now the right; at least, that upon the old rent and moderate fines they should be continued tenants to the Church, without any regard to those who had sold both their possession, and with that all the right or title that they might pretend to, for a valuable consideration. And they had the more hope of this, because the King had granted a commission, under the Great Seal of England to some Lords of the Council and to other eminent persons, to interpose and mediate with the bishops and clergy in such cases, as ought not to be prosecuted with rigour.

But the bishops and clergy concerned had not the good fortune to please their old or their new tenants. They had been very barbarously used themselves; and that had too much quenched all tenderness towards others. They did not enough distinguish between persons; nor did the suffering any man had undergone for fidelity to the King, or his affection to the church eminently expressed, often prevail for the mitigation of his fine; or if it did sometimes, three or four stories of the contrary, and in which there had been some unreasonable hardness used, made a greater noise and spread farther, than their examples of charity and moderation. And as honest men did not usually fare the better for any merit, so the purchasers who offered most money, did not fare the worse for all the villanies they had committed. And two or three unhappy instances of this kind brought scandal upon the whole Church, as if they had been all guilty of the same excesses, which they were far from.

The Life of Edward Earl of Clarendon, written by Himself, Oxford, 1761, II, pp. 184–5.

The New Pattern of Landownership

41 Edward Waterhouse, 1665

The Ways and Means of Raising Men and Families now in this Happy Return of Affairs in England

I proceed by the same blessed conduct, and under favour of the wise and pious, to suggest the ways and means of rises and decays of men and families now in England.... (The wars coming on, and those estates being out at interest and in trades trusted into several parts beyond the seas, and into this nation, wherein the late unhappy wars made garrisons of towns, and in the taking and re-taking of them, merchandise and staple goods portable became plundered by those, and such like courses, those personal estates of very great value became wholly lost or in a very great degree mutilated, and so the owners of them that way impoverished, unable to be afterwards either traders or increasers, or to give great portions with their children); so are we also to know that abundance of mean persons coming fresh into trade, the old traders being beaten out and ruined, or they being in offices of plunder, law, custom, trust of sale of Crown and bishops' lands, with such other courses of not dubious, but certainly illegal, title, did yet by their craft (knowing that Acts of Oblivion and Confirmation of Judicial Proceedings would come, as of course in all restitutions they do) so transfer their acquisitions of ill title into solid estate, that they raised themselves from nothing to great estate, and in that estate by small refundments, inconsiderable to what they thus indirectly acquired, established themselves in prosperity (while others that lost estates, and would get no new by those means, are in a great measure impoverished, and by reason thereof obscured. Such being the posture of things at home, and the affairs of those abroad requiring supply, few having wherewith but these traffickers in disturbance and otherwise casual gainers by it; they chiefly and in number must be the persons advantaged; nor is it strange to have money so requested and so operative to ingratiate men now; for the same feat it hath done in all revolutions. Solomon hence calls money a defence, Eccles. 7:12, and when we are told wisdom is good with an inheritance, we are to suspect that it little avails in worldly revolutions without it.

The Gentleman's Monitor, or a Sober Inspection into the Vertues, Vices, and Ordinary Means of the Rise and Decay of Men and Families, 1665, pp. 167, 169–70.

42   H.E. Chesney, 1932

It is hardly possible at present to estimate what proportion of the lands sold publicly during the Commonwealth were returned to their royalist owners at the Restoration. The returns from Crown lands up to 1667 would seem to indicate that many were not returned. But private sales alone justify the conclusion that the actual land settlement at the Restoration was a triumph for the 'new men'—men who may best be described not as Puritans but as business men who had thriven under the Commonwealth.

'The transference of lands in England, 1640–1660', *Transactions of the Royal Historical Society,* fourth series, xv, 1932, p. 210.

43   Joan Thirsk, 1954

At the first whisper of a restoration, Charles appears to have assumed that a full restoration of land would follow his return. In order to encourage his potential friends, he wrote to Mr Mordaunt in July 1659, promising compensation to all who made a timely show of loyalty to him for what they might lose by such a restoration. [See no. 35, p. 83.] Of the complexities of the land problem Charles and his advisers abroad at that time had no conception, since their information was gathered mainly from the propaganda of the anti-Commonwealth men. Dr John Barwick, writing from England that many landowners would exert themselves on Charles's behalf if they were certain of retaining their land purchases, was informed by Edward Hyde that the chief purchasers were irreconcilable parliamentarians, whom it would be useless to tempt with promises or favours. The view was naive and was soon dispelled. When, in later correspondence with General Monk, Charles described the land problem as one of the most perplexing with which he had to deal, facts had displaced legend. Charles then recognized that the recommendation that all sales should be confirmed was 'impossible and impracticable'. Yet might not a new confiscation imperil his throne? Had not Colonel Axtell, the regicide, threatened another civil war if the new owners were dispossessed?

Three different statements of policy made by Charles before his return to England mirrored his indecision. The first, of doubtful authenticity, contained a suggestion that purchasers of crown and church lands should surrender their estates but should first be given compensation for money paid out in excess of profits received. The second proposal, contained in a letter of uncertain date in the first half of 1660 from Charles to General Monk, suggested that all purchasers of confiscated land, including royalist land, should rest content with the profit they had already received. The third and final statement was included in the Declaration of Breda, where the whole problem of land sales was referred to parliament, and Charles undertook to accept its decisions. This announcement antagonized no one because it settled nothing. It contained none of the definite proposals put forward in Charles's private and semiofficial correspondence. But it had the great merit of absolving the king of the responsibility for one of the most vexatious of Restoration problems. Moreover, the earlier statements attributed to Charles on the subject had done good service. Charles had promised compensation for their losses to those who came over to his side quickly. He had also suggested compensation to the owners of crown and church lands. When the exact conditions of the settlement were discussed in parliament, it was customary to refer to the matter as the 'confirmation of sales', a term which encouraged the optimism of purchasers in the final verdict. An impression was thus successfully conveyed that both purchasers and former owners of confiscated land would be equally satisfied by the outcome.

One of the first bills presented to the Convention Parliament in May 1660 was a 'Bill touching land purchased from the trustees of the late parliament'. It preceded by several days the first reading of the bill of indemnity.... The bill was evidently sympathetic toward purchasers, but it seemed to advocate compensation to purchasers rather than a confirmation of sales. Speakers were evenly divided for and against.... Throughout the discussion, in so far as it was recorded, the financial interests of purchasers held pride of place, and no serious consideration was given to the proposal that they should be deprived of their land without recompense. At a later stage in the debate, for reasons not explained, royalist and crown lands were excluded from the scope of the bill. The amended version, applying to church lands only, was referred to a grand committee of the house, which was advised to pay some attention to the petitions of purchasers before it gave final shape to the bill. It was also instructed to consider the terms of compensation to be paid to the purchasers of crown lands. The terms offered to both groups of owners were evidently intended to follow similar lines.

At this time both houses of parliament were giving consideration to two kindred matters—the bill of indemnity and oblivion and the bill for the confirmation of judicial proceedings.... The Act for the Confirmation of Judicial Proceedings had a direct bearing on the subject. Former owners of confiscated land needed some safeguard that they would not be debarred by the terms of the act from recovering their property, when once parliament indicated the means. They were pacified with three clauses: nothing in the act was to be construed to confirm or invalidate sales carried out by the treason trustees; any person who was liable to suffer serious wrong by the confirmation of fines, recoveries, and other sentences at law dating from the Interregnum might appeal for a remedy by writ of error or some other accepted procedure, exactly as he would have done in normal circumstances; the failure of persons whose estates had been compulsorily sold to make such an appeal was not to prejudice their right to the land, so long as they prosecuted their claims by way of an action at law, or by lawful entry, within five years after May 29, 1660.

These three clauses suggested to all dispossessed owners a way of redress in the common-law courts. But they were not regarded as the final and complete solution of the land problem. The task of restoring crown and church lands and of satisfying the claims of former tenants and purchasers became a matter for a royal commission, while royalists with sufficient influence had recourse to private acts. Moreover, parliament continued its discussions on the bill for sales. In short, the clauses in the Act for the Confirmation of Judicial Proceedings were treated rather as a warning to purchasers than as a final judgment on the claims of the dispossessed. They suggested a method of recovering land by legal action, but they did not close the door to other methods.

The energy with which parliament first tackled the bill for sales was quickly spent. Finding a way to satisfy purchasers proved more difficult than was anticipated, and on August 6, 1660 the committee appointed to settle the matter turned once more to the commons for advice. The house was bankrupt of ideas and proposed that representatives of the church and purchasers should themselves suggest a satisfactory settlement. In the meantime, legislation was passed to prevent church landlords from issuing new leases until the bill for sales was passed.

Before further time could be given to the bill, the king proposed a parliamentary recess, and on September 13 the house ended its sittings until November 6. On the day before they dispersed, the commons and lords suggested that during their absence the king should set up a commission under the great seal to treat with purchasers of church lands. If fair terms could not be decided between the two parties, the principles of an agreement were to be presented to parliament on its return. This decision, coupled with the one made earlier that owners and purchasers of church lands should suggest their own terms of settlement, proved to be the first step toward a new solution—one which obviated the need for a legislative settlement....

The commission was announced in a proclamation of October 7, 1660.... The commissioners were named and their tasks enumerated. They were to collect the names of all purchasers of land; information on the prices they had paid, how much money had been paid in cash and how much in bills, how many bills had been proved to be forgeries; what profits had been made from rents and resales, timber cutting, and improvements; which purchasers had bought because they were tenants and which had bought for gain. The commissioners were authorized to summon anyone to give evidence who held documents and information relating to the sales. The inquiry was to embrace both crown and church lands, but not delinquents' lands. Since the information would take some time to collect, the proclamation informed purchasers of crown lands that they might collect all arrears of rent, including those due at Michaelmas. A week later, a letter was dispatched from the king to the Archbishop of Canterbury, expressing his wish that those who had been tenants and purchasers of church lands should receive considerate treatment in the grant of leases [see no. 39, p. 88]. The clergy were asked to give priority in the issue of leases to former tenants but, in the case of land sold under the Commonwealth to members of the army, to refrain from issuing any leases for the time being, except to former purchasers or their assigns.

When once parliament resumed its sittings, all petitions from purchasers were handed to the commissioners. The bill for sales, however, remained under discussion by the grand committee of the house. Andrew Marvell, reporting progress to the Hull city council, described the concern of the commons to get the bill through as quickly as possible.... Yet on December 4, Andrew Marvell wrote no longer of eagerness but of lack of inclination to pass the bill. The explanation came from other sources. The commissioners appointed by Charles II were functioning very satisfactorily: *Mercurius Publicus* commented on the satisfaction of both purchasers and former owners; the lord chancellor at the dissolution on December 29 expressed the same view, adding that the commission would continue its work pending the election of the new chamber. In view of its success, both houses of parliament were more than ready to leave the matter in its hands.

When the Cavalier Parliament assembled in May 1661, the lord chancellor made no reference to the land problem. The omission was significant because it had earned comment in all earlier speeches. It was a sign that the issue was regarded as settled. One year after the restoration of the king the matter had abruptly ceased to command attention. The bill for sales was not revived, and no more time was spent on legislation relating to the land settlement.

The protracted discussions that had taken place in parliament had been almost entirely confined to the subject of public lands.

Apart from establishing the principle that forfeited land should be restored to its former owners, they brought little comfort to private royalists. Parliament had made it clear that it was not prepared to consider general legislation on their behalf. They were recommended instead to prosecute a claim for recovery within five years in a court of law. . . .

Members of the nobility found an answer in private acts. In the words of Lord Craven's petition, this was a means to 'avoid multiplicity of suits'. The house of lords gave the bills a ready hearing, but they were not so well received in the commons. In the first place, the house was fully occupied in discussing bills of a general nature. In the second, we know, on the authority of Clarendon, that private bills caused much acrimonious debate. They threatened to defeat the aim of the king that recriminations in public concerning the events of the Interregnum should cease. Charles watched closely the passage of these private bills and, in at least one instance, took action to prevent the passing of a bill which had caused much wrangling. In the third place, the marked increase in the number of private bills denoted a tendency, which displeased Charles as much as it, no doubt, displeased the lawyers, to expand the role of parliament as a court of equity. The king's objections were explicitly stated at the prorogation of the Cavalier Parliament in May 1662. But they were in evidence long before this and may have contributed to the early death of many private bills. Of fifty royalists owning land in the southeastern counties, only the Duke of Newcastle, Lord Colepeper, and Lord Arundel obtained private acts.

The sympathy of the house of lords found an outlet instead in a series of orders, which, in straightforward cases, were as effective in restoring the land of the nobility as private acts. The orders were dispatched to the sheriffs in the counties, instructing them to put delinquents in possession of their land. Little resistance was encountered from purchasers, partly, no doubt, as Clarendon explained, because they recognized the measure as one of the king's obligations to his followers, partly also because resistance was fruitless. Those who were obstructive were taken into custody until they submitted.

Private acts and orders of the house of lords solved the problems of a minority—of eight out of a sample of fifty royalists with land in southeastern England. The remainder, however, did not present so large a problem as their numbers might suggest, for some had recovered their property before 1660. Nineteen out of fifty royalists (38 per cent) had managed before 1660 to buy back 45 out of their 179 properties (25 per cent). The situation was quite different from that obtaining on crown and church lands, where no undercover restitution of land had been possible before 1660. These facts partly justify parliament's lack of policy on the subject of private lands. The problem was small compared with that presented by public lands.

Cast upon their own resources, royalists sometimes succeeded in reaching private agreements with purchasers outside the courts of law. . . .

Royalists who failed to secure a private act or a private agreement applied to the courts for a writ of trespass and ejectment. . . . Although it has proved impossible to find many of these lawsuits in the records of the courts, there is no doubt that the majority of royalists successfully regained their land.

Seventy per cent of the properties which were sold under the Commonwealth in southeastern England have been traced back to their owners in 1660, and further enquiry would probably yield more. Thus, forty-five out of 179 estates were recovered before 1660, and at least 81 afterwards. Royalists regained their land in all but exceptional circumstances.

A suit at law was likely to fail only when royalists had prejudiced their titles by confirming sales to purchasers during the Interregnum. Such confirmatory releases, which had been obtained by purchasers at a price, were treated by parliament as 'voluntary sales', which could not be undone. They came into the same category as the private sales by which royalists had raised money in order to compound for their delinquency. . . .

The key to the terms of the settlement relating to crown and church lands lay in the decision appointing commissioners to investigate in detail the accounts of Commonwealth purchasers. A report was demanded of every penny received and paid out in connection with forfeited land, and from this report commissioners were expected to have little difficulty in deciding whether purchasers deserved compensation or not. As we have already seen, the duties of the commissioners did not extend to the examination of transactions relating to delinquents' estates. Nevertheless, when financial disputes between delinquents and purchasers came into the court of chancery, they were dealt with in exactly the same way. When the Duke of Buckingham claimed his estate from the Commonwealth purchaser, Francis Dodsworth, in 1659, the judgment provided for a full inquiry into the profits and expenditures of the latter.

It is fair to assume that a large number of purchasers of crown and church lands received no compensation whatever because their profits during the Interregnum had been more than adequate and that purchasers of delinquents' lands who resigned their interests without protest did so because they knew that no appeals of hardship would stand up to a scrutiny as severe as that carried out by the king's commissioners and the chancery judges.

'The Restoration land settlement', *Journal of Modern History,* XXVI, no. 4, 1954, 315–24, 326.

44   H. J. Habakkuk, 1965

During the Interregnum the state appropriated and sold the property of the Crown, of the Church and of those royalists who were unable or ineligible to compound for their delinquency and so regain possession of their estates by paying a fine. By acquiring such property some new landowners appeared in the countryside. But at the Restoration the sales of confiscated property were invalidated. Some purchasers of Crown and Church property stayed on after 1660 as leaseholders, but the number appears to have been small; as to the sales of the confiscated estates of the private royalists, all I know confirms Mrs Thirsk's conclusion that 'royalists regained their land in all but exceptional circumstances'[1].

The burden of the argument that the land transactions of this period led to permanent changes seems, therefore, to fall upon the royalists whose estates were sequestrated—not confiscated— and who paid a fine to compound for their delinquency and so regained possession of their property. Such royalists had sometimes to sell land in order to raise money for their fines and such

---

[1] J. Thirsk, 'The Restoration Land Settlement', *Journal of Modern History,* XXVI, no. 4 (Dec. 1954), p. 323. See above, pp. 92–9.

sales, which in form at least were voluntary, were not undone at the Restoration. It has been commonly suggested that a large amount of land was sold under private contracts made for this purpose. 'Much land', writes Mr Hill, 'passed by private sale into the hands of those with ready cash.' In the same context Sir Keith Feiling refers to Clarendon allowing 'a vast mass of property to remain in Puritan hands' at the Restoration.[2]...

In order to assess the effect of the Civil Wars I have investigated the history of 32 royalists who held property in Northamptonshire and Bedfordshire and who paid fines for delinquency. This geographical limitation clearly circumscribes the validity of any conclusions, but there is no reason to believe that the royalists of this area fared better than those of the north and west or that their experience is unrepresentative.

In the case of all the royalists examined, the debts which led to sales on a large scale were incurred *before*, not during or after, the Civil War.... The royalists were prepared to part with plate and jewels but they did not seem willing—or if willing were not able—to charge their estates for the royal cause.... Where there *were* large royalist sales, therefore, these were not, to any significant extent, to meet debts incurred to help the king. They were primarily to meet debts incurred before the war; the most extensive sales were, in fact, made under arrangements entered into before 1642.

About half the families examined had substantial debts.... Where no formal provision had been made before the civil war for the repayment of creditors, the war and its aftermath gave the creditor every incentive to enter upon the land of his royalist debtor. The details of the procedure varied according to the nature of the debt, but the main sequence of events is the same. When the local sequestration committee took over the delinquent's estates, the creditors by due legal process moved in, to safeguard their own interest....

But whether or not the royalist families which had entered the war with a heavy burden of debt were more or less heavily indebted by 1660, many of them found themselves at the Restoration with a part of their estates still in the hands of creditors, or at least with a substantial portion of the income of their estates assigned for

---

[2] C. Hill, *Puritanism and Revolution*, 1958, p. 167; K.G. Feiling, *A History of England from the Coming of the English to 1918*, 1950, p. 540. See also the same author's *A History of the Tory Party, 1640–1714*, Oxford, 1924, p. 101.

the payment of their debts. Some of these families who had been unable or unwilling to sell during the Interregnum because of the political uncertainties, now parted with some property. Others, though they avoided sale, remained under heavy pressure from their creditors. It is the discontent arising from these circumstances that explains the importance which the royalists attached to their sufferings during the Interregnum and in particular to the composition fines. It was natural that families should attribute to the events after 1642 misfortunes which were already implicit in their economic circumstances before the war, and that the fines should become the focus for a wide range of discontents. The royalists in 1660 were aggrieved, less because of the land they had been forced to sell in the 1640's and 1650's than because their estates were still in the hands of their creditors; it was not the memory of the sales they had made, so much as the sales they were being forced to make in the 1660's, that sharpened their sense of grievance.

There is a final reservation to be made. Not only has the burden of the fine been exaggerated in individual cases; those who were fined at all were only a minority of the landowning class. About 3,225 persons compounded for their delinquency. According to Gregory King there were in 1688 15,560 families of the rank of gentry and above. Thus, even on the assumption that all those who compounded were in fact landowners in King's sense, only about a fifth of the gentry and higher social groups compounded for their estates.... The active Royalists were therefore a minority. Indeed, the royalists and parliamentarians taken together were no more than a minority, for there were fewer parliamentarians than royalists among the nobility and gentry. A majority of English landowners were neutral. We cannot, of course, from these figures know how many of the substantial landowners committed themselves....

Some revolutionary régimes have produced major changes in the distribution of property, and it is natural to suppose from the impositions and confiscations of the Interregnum that the Commonwealth and Protectorate did so. Perhaps if the Civil Wars had taken place half a century earlier, they would have had profound effects on landownership in England. But by the 1640's, the royalists' estates were protected by institutions which had developed in the decades before the war broke out. In the later sixteenth century the market in mortgages had developed, partly as a result of the legislation which made it no longer a criminal offence to take interest at or below the rate of 10 per cent; contacts between lenders and borrowers were quickened, so that a royalist could borrow the money for his fine instead of being forced to sell property. A second development which proved to protect the royalists was the recognition, by the Courts, in the 1620's, of the debtor's equity of redemption; without this, the creditors who occupied a royalist's estate, when he defaulted on his debt, would have automatically acquired full ownership. Thirdly the gradual elaboration of forms of family settlement also mitigated the burden of the exactions of the Interregnum on the family estate in certain instances. It was these developments, rather than any particular leniency in the treatment of royalists which explains why the Interregnum had so little effect on the distribution of property.

'Landowners and the Civil War', *Economic History Review*, 2nd ser., XVIII, no. 1, 1965, pp. 130–1, 143–4, 147–8.

New Attitudes to Land

45 Duchess of Newcastle, 1667

The Duchess describes her husband s return to his estates in 1660

Thus he kissed his Majesty's hand, and went the next day into Nottinghamshire, to his manor-house called Welbeck; but when he came there, and began to examine his estate, and how it had been ordered in the time of his banishment, he knew not whether he had left anything of it for himself or not, till by his prudence and wisdom he informed himself the best he could, examining those that had most knowledge therein. Some lands, he found, could be recovered no further than for his life, and some not at all; some had been in the rebels' hands, which he could not recover, but by his Highness the Duke of York's favour, to whom his Majesty had given all the estates of those that were condemned and executed for murdering his Royal Father of blessed memory, which by the law were forfeited to his Majesty; whereof his Highness graciously restored my Lord so much of the land that formerly had been his, as amounted to £730 a year.[1] . . .

After my Lord had begun to view those ruins that were nearest, and tried the law to keep or recover what formerly was his (which certainly showed no favour to him, besides that the Act of Oblivion proved a great hindrance and obstruction to those his designs, as it did no less to all the royal party), and had settled so much of his estate as possibly he could, he cast up the sum of his debts, and set out several parts of land for the payment of them, or of

---

[1] The Duchess omits to mention that on 13 Sept. 1660, Charles II gave his assent to a private Act 'for restoring to William, Marquis of Newcastle, all his Honours, Manors, Lands, and Tenements in England, whereof he was in possession on the 20th day of May 1640, or at any time since'. This Act, however, would not touch lands sold or mortgaged by Newcastle himself.

some of them (for some of his lands could not be easily sold, being entailed) and some he sold in Derbyshire to buy the Castle of Nottingham, which, although it is quite ruined and demolished, yet, it being a seat which had pleased his father very much, he would not leave it since it was offered to be sold.

His two houses, Welbeck and Bolsover, he found much out of repair, and this later half pulled down; no furniture or any necessary goods were left in them, but some few hangings and pictures, which had been saved by the care and industry of his eldest daughter the Lady Cheiny, and were bought over again after the death of his eldest son Charles, Lord Mansfield. For they being given to him, and he leaving some debts to be paid after his death, my Lord sent to his other son Henry, now Earl of Ogle, to endeavour for so much credit, that the said hangings and pictures (which my Lord esteemed very much, the pictures being drawn by Van Dyke) might be saved; which he also did, and my Lord hath paid the debt since his return.

Of eight parks, which my Lord had before the wars, there was but one left that was not quite destroyed, viz. Welbeck Park, of about four miles' compass. . . .

Thus, though his lawsuits and other unavoidable expenses were very chargeable to him, yet he ordered his affairs so prudently, that by degrees he stocked and manured those lands he keeps for his own use, and in part repaired his manor-houses, Welbeck and Bolsover, to which latter he made some additional building; and though he has not yet built the seat at Nottingham, yet he hath stocked and paled a little park belonging to it.

The Life of William Cavendish, Duke of Newcastle, by Margaret, Duchess of Newcastle, ed. C.H. Firth, 1907, pp. 69–72.

46   Ian Gentles, 1971

At the Restoration, when the condition of the Crown estates came under the searching scrutiny of the surveyor-general, Sir Charles Harbord, and the county surveyors under him, the behaviour of the soldiers was the subject of severe recriminations, but most of the civilian purchasers escaped without reproach. Only one instance has been discovered where a civilian purchaser presided over the destruction of a royal manor house. It occurred at Langton Herring, Dorset, where the house was torn down and the materials sold. But Viscount William Monson, the purchaser of the manor, charged that the act of destruction had been performed by William and Alice Biles, who had been in unlawful possession of the house. In most other cases about which information has been found the civilians showed pride in their record as landholders and drew attention to the improvements they had made and the capital expenses they had incurred. Several of them wrote to Sir Charles Harbord rationalizing their co-operation with the 'late usurpers' as springing from a desire to preserve the royal estates from waste and depredation. In most cases Harbord accepted their claims without cavil, and they were permitted to continue as tenants of the king with generous leases.

Military purchasers

With the notable exception of John Lambert, most of the Parliamentary officers have received a bad press for their stewardship of the Crown lands....

Many of the officers of course did nothing but draw the income from their holdings. The majority of the Crown lands had already been let out on long leases, and frequently the soldiers were content to allow the lessees quiet possession in return for regular payment of rent. Other soldiers, however, were not satisfied to draw a modest income in this fashion, but insisted upon increasing their return. Ready cash could be obtained in several ways. When an estate was rich in woodland the timber could be cut and the deer killed. A park could be 'disparked'—converted to arable or pasture—and let for a higher rent. A large estate could be subdivided into small holdings, whose total yield would be higher than the original unfragmented rent. A large mansion house or lodge could be stripped of its lead, for which there was always a high demand, or it could be completely dismantled and all the materials—stone, glass, and wood in particular—carted off and auctioned.... It is known that after the Restoration the revenues from Crown lands shrank to a fraction of their former size. It has been implied that some of this shrinkage was due to the depredations which had occurred during the 'usurpation'. However, the extent of these depredations was frequently exaggerated by men who had good reason for doing so. At the same time soldiers were blamed for destruction which had occurred either before they took over the estates or in 1659–60, when their authority was no longer respected by their tenants. . . .

It is important to remember, that a good proportion of the destruction of Crown timber, about which his Majesty's surveyors were so vocal in 1660, was not the work of soldiers but a consequence of the official policy of the Commonwealth and Protectorate. Exact figures for the amount of timber reserved for the navy are not known, but it is known that on some large estates virtually all the good timber was reserved in this way. . . .

A final phase of destruction for which the soldiers cannot be held responsible accompanied the chaos and disorder surrounding the Restoration. Whether motivated by a desire for royalist vengeance or by simple opportunism, many people took the return of Charles II as the signal for an attack upon the property of the hapless soldiers. . . .

Perhaps the most detailed account of destruction that occurred at the Restoration was left by Captain Adam Baynes. In his correspondence is a paper entitled, 'A Perticular or Estimate of the Losse and Damage which did Accrew to Mr Baynes. . .in Holdenby . . .1661'. It itemizes the losses of wood, deer, and fish which were inflicted upon him by his under tenants, to the value of £70. They had also flouted his orders by ploughing up 182 acres of pasture before the last Lady Day. Baynes had lost all the grass that might have grown there at the rate of 2s. an acre, and he had also been 'preiudiced in his Stocke for want thereof.' In an appended statement Robert Baynes asserted that the under tenants had trampled on the rest of Baynes's pasture when they went every day to plough their 182 acres. The total damage was said to amount to £112. In addition, the under tenants were withholding their rents to the sum of £198 16s. od., 'many of them refusinge to pay him upon pretence that they did not enjoy theire bargaines.' If Baynes's experience is at all typical the Parliamentary purchasers must have had a trying time of it immediately after the overthrow of the Protectorate. . . .

At Theobalds in Hertfordshire, not only was the face of the property changed but a small community of republicans was established there, whose unity of social and religious ideas brought them some notoriety. . . . The park and palace were acquired by the officers of Thomas Fairfax's horse regiment, and several of them took up residence there under the leadership of Major William Packer. The result was that Theobalds, 'from [being] the seat of a monarch...[became] a little commonwealth; so many entire tenements, like splinters, [having] flown out of the materials thereof.' The thirty acres belonging to the palace were divided into many small plots, and the palace itself was then demolished and the materials used to build tenement houses upon the plots. The park was similarly subdivided, enclosed, and built upon. Of the occupants, six were army officers, but at least two dozen more were civilians. The community found its focus in a radical Baptist chapel which scandalized some of the local inhabitants, and proved to be a thorn in the side of the government.

That the soldiers caused drastic alterations in the appearance and use of the Crown lands is not to be doubted; that this fact demonstrates reckless or wanton exploitation on their part is a different question. It is important to remember that the soldiers' needs were not the same as the king's, and that therefore it was reasonable for them to dismantle and sell things for which they had no use. Only occasionally would there be a soldier like John Lambert, who desired a royal palace. There were few others who could afford to maintain such immense edifices. Accordingly, at Richmond, Oatlands, Berkhamsted, Holdenby, and Theobalds, they tore them down and either sold the materials or used them to build more practical structures. The fate of these fabrics paralleled that of the monasteries in the sixteenth century. In both cases the old buildings disappeared because they did not suit the needs of the new purchasers....

These alterations in land use sometimes entailed sizeable capital investments. Such investments were frequently mentioned in the petitions of soldiers who sought permission at the Restoration to continue in possession of their estates.... Windsor Great Park was the subject of a petition in 1660 from Captain Edward Scotton, Captain Robert Aldridge, Richard Southwood, and John Scotton, who were in possession of part of the park. They declared that they had expended 'great somes of mony in improveing the same;' yet that autumn their corn and hay had been seized for his Majesty's use. Accompanying the petition was a 'supplication...of the purchasers and possessors,' outlining the improvements they had undertaken. They had paid fifteen years' purchase for the park, and had then subdivided it into about 100 parcels which they had enclosed with hedges and ditches 'att the great charge of the said purchasers and possessors.'...

The fact that two of the most important works on agriculture in the seventeenth century were written by Parliamentary officers who bought Crown land contributes to the general argument that in their management of the Crown lands the soldiers were in accord with the mainstream of progressive agricultural thinking of the previous century and a half. To be sure, not all the soldiers were improvers; nor did those who were attempt to implement the more grandiose schemes of the theorists. But it is still fair to say that by and large they were rational and often progressive land managers.

The soldiers' behaviour makes good economic sense when it is remembered that the prices they had paid for their estates were reasonable only on the assumption that the lands would be used for purposes different from those which the king had favoured. One can therefore dismiss the traditional view of Cromwell's soldiers as the wanton destroyers of the Crown estates and judge them instead as energetic, if often ruthless, agrarian developers.

'The management of the Crown Lands, 1649–1660', *Agricultural History Review*, XIX, no. 1, 1971, pp. 25–8, 30–2, 35–8, 40–1.

47   Christopher Hill, 1949

The restoration, then, was by no means a restoration of the old order. The King and the bishops came back indeed from their travels, even had some of their lands returned to them. But the old agrarian relationships had been shattered, and with them the social basis of the Stuart monarchy as it existed before 1640. Even before the policy of selling delinquents' lands was adopted the county sequestration committees had been subject to continual bullying from the Committee at Goldsmith's Hall to 'improve' the lands in their charge. Crown lands were similarly squeezed by order of Parliament (February 15, 1647–48). After the restoration it was noted that revenue from the custody of the royal parks had increased ten- or twenty-fold. Even where the previous owners got their lands back after 1660, they could no longer manage them on the same conditions. Where there had been outright confiscation and sale, or in the probably more numerous cases of private sale by indigent royalist landowners, the speculator had descended on the land, buying estates in order to reorganize, enclose, rack rents, and then sell again at a profit. Many purchasers were interested only in quick returns, being no doubt like Mr Highland who re-sold lands he had purchased, 'suspicious lest the tide should turn.'

When the restoration took place, then, church, crown and delinquent lands had been for a decade or more in the occupation of farmers who had bought or leased them as a financial proposition, and so had made the most they could out of them; it was hence impossible to restore the semi-feudal conditions of land-holding on these estates. Land had of necessity become primarily a source of money income even for the restored royalist. Selden noted the logic of the new society when he said: 'When men did let their lands under foot [i.e., below their true value], the tenants would fight for their landlords, so that way they had their retribution; but now they will do nothing for them, may be the first, if but a constable bid them, that shall lay the landlord by the heels, and therefore 'tis vanity and folly not to take the full value.' The bishops drew the same conclusion. After the restoration they used to get together to work out a policy to govern their relations with their tenants. Bishop Cosin of Durham, who very closely followed his land agent's dealings with the tenants of the diocese, used to quote the practice of other bishops in the matter of rents and fines and leases for lives and suggested that he would be liable to criticism if he violated their agreed policy.

Church and crown lands had remained undeveloped before 1640, not so much out of principle (though the theorists of these institutions, like most theorists, sometimes tried to make a virtue of their necessities) as because their owners had never possessed the capital to invest in 'improvements.' That stage was surmounted in the fifties, and when they were restored the former owners reaped the benefit. Delinquents' lands were only partially restored, the great mass of estates which had changed hands by private sale were not restored at all, so that there it was even less possible to return to the old ways.

'Land in the English Revolution', *Science and Society*, XIII, no. 1, 1948–49, pp. 46–7.

Part Four

ECONOMIC POLICY AND ECONOMIC DEVELOPMENT

Economic policy

Until the Restoration all seventeenth-century writers on economic matters focused their attention on trade as the main source of the nation's wealth and wellbeing. The Duke of Newcastle's advice to Charles II (48) stated in the simplest terms the general view. 'Your Majesty will be pleased to keep up the merchant', he advised. But how was this to be done, when even the merchants were deeply divided among themselves? The Duke of Newcastle did not touch the tangled problem of what policy would best promote this end, but it lay at the centre of pamphlets written by the professional economic writers at this time, and, indeed, continued a controversy that had been raging since the mid-sixteenth century. A regulated trade had been the general rule since Tudor times; its defenders preferred prosperity in conjunction with orderliness. But an ordered trade meant regulations which selected a group of privileged traders; those rejected were for ever aggrieved. The latter, therefore, upheld the opposing view that the public interest was best served by free trade.

Samuel Fortrey's essay, first published in 1663 (49), laid much emphasis on the role of the state and the monarch in promoting the nation's prosperity. Although some of his recommended measures involved the lifting of restraints on trade, the passage selected here shows that the fundamental principle underlying the suggested policy was not complete economic freedom. He offered an ingenious argument in defence of a regulated trade in companies. Roger Coke (50) while insisting on peace as an essential requirement of a prosperous economy, also protested loudly in favour of free trade. But on closer reading, it is clear that his conception of free trade likewise called for a certain amount of state intervention. In short, state building through trade, that is to say mercantilism, was being ever more carefully defined and refined.

Coke's main themes represent those of many other contemporary writers. The Dutch example was extremely influential in moulding opinion and in shifting the interest of the policy-builders from trade to industry, and thence to a host of related matters. Sir Josiah Child's evidence to the *Lords Committee on the Decay of Rents and Trade* (1669) illustrates this train of thought (54). The clerk's notes conveniently summarize what Child said on that occasion, but they can be read in their expanded form in his *Brief Considerations concerning Trade and Interest of Money* (1668). The sources of many of Child's ideas were four pamphlets, three of which were published in 1641, 1651, and 1657. They have been analysed, and their principle ideas tabulated by W. Letwin (55), who effectively demonstrates how theorists at the Restoration were not attempting to reverse earlier policies, but only developing them further.

The success of the Dutch in opening their doors to foreigners and thereby establishing new industries based on imported foreign skills taught important lessons in England, which are a theme in the essays of Roger Coke and Josiah Child. But Carew Reynel (51) was the most adventurous and open-minded thinker on this score. His writing reflected the driving energy of enterprising traders and industrialists, who saw infinite possibilities of economic improvement ahead. Like other writers, his propaganda was not directed towards advancing the interests of one class only, but benefiting the nation in general. But he was more alert than many to those projects which created plenty of employment for the poor. On these grounds, he even advocated tobacco-growing which had been prohibited by government since 1619. No one else considered such a major reversal of policy.

In 1680 the anonymous writer of *Britannia Languens* (52) considered more earnestly than before the possibility that some disproportionately influential private interests could so conflict with the public benefit as to beget general economic depression. This possibility had not been discussed so directly in earlier literature, though it was touched on by Carew Reynel, but now it was brought out into the open at a time when deep concern was felt for the sluggishness of trade. This discussion forms a bridge between the arguments of men such as Fortrey and Adam

Smith. Smith, writing in 1776 (though his ideas had been taking shape in lectures since 1750) came round to the view that under a mercantilist system some private interests could exercise such inordinate influence at the expense of other private interests, that ultimately they injured the majority. Hence his advocacy of a much freer trade, involving little or no state intervention (53). Smith's 'belief in the economic beneficence of self-interest', wrote Edwin Cannan in 1904, 'has afforded a starting ground for economic speculation ever since'.[1]

Economic development

Some contemporaries noted the thrusting power of the newly invigorated economy at the Restoration. Houghton's description of agricultural improvement has been much quoted (57). But not everyone agreed that it dated from the Restoration; some traced it back to earlier years, especially the 1650s (56). Nor did all agree that the benefits reached all classes. The Reverend Richard Baxter who saw the rural scene from the small husbandman's viewpoint was passionately concerned for the hardships of farm tenants (58).

William Cunningham saw at the Restoration an 'exuberant development of national life' and a wave of commercial expansion, which, in his view, had been lacking under Cromwell. He also attributed to the Restoration government responsibility for strengthening and stiffening the mercantile system.[2] In his view, this system of state building through trade also entailed the destruction of all government machinery for providing help for the poor and sick, and encouraged business men to strive harder for profit and forget compassion. His interpretation of economic policy at the Restoration as mercantilist in purpose and selfishly individualist in its business philosophy is substantially reiterated by two twentieth-century historians, Dr Lipson and Dr Christopher Hill (59, 60). But on the ancestry of this mercantile policy, and the rigour of its impact on the working classes, their emphasis differs. Both see many innovations in the economic policy of the Commonwealth, which had a fresh outlook on economic life and unleashed

---

[1] Adam Smith, *The Wealth of Nations*, ed. Edwin Cannan, 6th edition, Methuen University Paperback, 1961, p. xli.

[2] W. Cunningham, *The Growth of English Industry and Commerce in Modern Times. Part I. The Mercantile System*, 1919, pp. 201–6.

forces of drive, energy, and enthusiasm which could not be stayed after 1660. At the same time Dr Lipson blames on the war and the Commonwealth government the breakdown of the paternal authoritarian framework that had curbed individualism under the old monarchy. Henceforward, the pursuit of private profit could not be restrained by governments. Dr Hill presents the legacy of the Interregnum less harshly, seeing 'healthy industrial growth' (though he is quoting Professor Hughes here) in the liberation of industry and trade during the Interregnum,[3] but seeing a change of basic philosophy at the Restoration which turned this liberty into the ugly pursuit of private profit at the cost of the labouring classes. Charles Wilson (61) sees policy at the Restoration as a revised version of old principles and policies that were already in evidence in the 1620s, which continued to dominate policy during the Interregnum and were refurbished and improved after 1660 in the light of changing facts and past lessons. His examples relate to trade especially, though also to industry, and agriculture. The result in his view was a mature mercantile policy after 1660 which, was, however, always ready to mould itself to the changing pattern of trade and industry. It did not advance individuals at the expense of the nation but struck a considered balance between them.

A brisk paragraph by Professor Caroline Robbins succinctly sums up the economic mood and economic consequences of the Restoration (62).

[3] Christopher Hill, *The Century of Revolution*, pp. 145–6.

The Role of the State in fostering Economic Prosperity

48 The Duke of Newcastle, 1660

It is the merchant that only brings honey to the hive.... Therefore your Majesty will be pleased to keep up the merchant that can only fill your kingdom with riches, and so consequently enrich your Majesty; for if your kingdom be poor, where can your Majesty have it? Nowhere. Therefore your Majesty will be pleased to enrich your kingdom that neither your Majesty nor your subjects may want, and that is done absolutely by the merchant and only by the merchant.

Clarendon MS 109, f. 41, Bodleian Library, Oxford.

49 Samuel Fortrey, 1663

Two things therefore appear to be chiefly necessary, to make a nation great and powerful; which is to be rich, and populous; and this nation enjoying together all those advantages with part whereof only, others grow great and flourishing; and withal, a Prince, who above all things delights and glories in his people's happiness: this nation can expect no less than to become the most great, and flourishing of all others.

But private advantages are often impediments of public profit; for in what any single person shall be a loser, there, endeavours will be made to hinder the public gain, from whence proceeds the ill success that commonly attends the endeavours for public good; for commonly it is but coldly prosecuted, because the benefit may possibly be something remote from them that promote it; but the mischief known and certain to them that oppose it: and interest more than reason commonly sways most men's affections.

Whereby it may appear how necessary it is that the public profits should be in a single power to direct, whose interest is only the benefit of the whole.

The greatest thing therefore that any Prince can aim at, is to make his dominions rich and populous, and by what means it may be effected in this nation, beyond all neighbour countries, I shall endeavour to demonstrate: people and plenty are commonly the begetters the one of the other, if rightly ordered.

And first, to increase the people of this nation, permission would be given to all people of foreign countries, under such restrictions as the state shall think fit, freely to inhabit and reside within this kingdom, with liberty to buy or sell lands or goods, to import or export any commodities, with the like privilege and freedom that English men have.

In the next place, our manufactures are to be considered, on which chiefly depends both the wealth and prosperity of this kingdom: for by the increase and encouragement thereof, the subjects are employed in honest and industrious callings, maintained and preserved from want, and those mischiefs which commonly attend idleness: the people furnished at home with all things both of necessity and pleasure; and by the overplus procure from abroad, whatever for use or delight is wanting.

The chief manufactures amongst us at this day are only woollen clothes, woollen stuff of all sorts, stockings, ribbandings, and perhaps some few silk stuffs, and some other small things, scarce worth naming; and these already named so decayed and adulterated, that they are almost out of esteem both at home and abroad.

And this, because foreign commodities are grown into so great esteem amongst us, as we wholly undervalue and neglect the use of our own, whereby that great expense of treasure, that is yearly wasted in clothing, furnitures, and the like, redounds chiefly to the profit of strangers, and to the ruin of his Majesty's subjects. . . .

But most of these evils would be easily prevented, if only his Majesty would be pleased to commend to his people, by his own example, the esteem and value he hath of his own commodities, in which the greatest Courtier may be as honourably clad, as in the best dress, Paris, or a French tailor can put him in; besides it seems to be more honourable for a King of England rather to become a pattern to his own people, than to conform to the humours and fancies of other nations; especially when it is so much to his prejudice.

This alone, without further trouble, would be at least ten hundred thousand pounds a year to the advantage of his people; for the courtiers always endeavour to imitate the Prince, being desirous to obtain his favour, which they can no way better do, than by approving his actions in being of like humour: and the Court being the copy that the gentry strive to write after, and the rest of the people commonly follow; it appears of what great consequence and advantage the good example of a Prince is to the benefit of his people....

In the next place concerning our trade abroad with strangers: and this would also be encouraged, and increased by all means possible, and when any commodity is raised to the greatest height it is capable of, it should be free for exportation, under so reasonable customs, that the merchant may afford his commodity abroad, as cheap as others, or else he would not be able to vent it.

Secondly, all foreign commodities that are useful to improve our own manufactures and trade abroad, and cannot be raised here, should be brought unto us under easy customs, the better to enable us, at an easy exchange, to vent our commodities abroad.

Thirdly, all foreign commodities whatsoever that are only useful to be spent within the nation, and that have already all their perfection, as fruits, sugars, wines, linen cloth, laces, silks, and what else can receive no addition here, and are not to be again transported; such commodities should pay extraordinary customs, but should not be forbidden to be brought in; for by this means, these commodities will be so dear to the people, that it will much wean them from so lavish an use of them, as might otherwise be, and for such things as we are capable to raise, it will much increase it of our own; whereby the State will raise a good revenue, and the country save their wealth, that would be wastefully spent abroad, and so increase our own manufactures at home.

Fourthly, the increase of our land in any kind (except sheep alive and mares) that have already all the perfection that we can add unto them, should be free for exportation, under reasonable customs; and of all things this nation is capable to raise, there is not any one of so great profit, as the exportation of horses, which of all commodities is of least charge to be raised at home, and of greatest value abroad.

There yet remains something to be said concerning merchants, associating themselves in companies; the benefit or prejudice whereof hath been often controverted, but something difficult to determine.

It is true, that it is opposed by many, conceiving the free liberty of trade would be much more advantageous in the general, because these companies, keeping the trade to themselves only, will have what commodities are to be vented abroad at their own price, and at an under-value; none having occasion to buy them but themselves: whereby the workmen are many times discouraged, and sometimes undone. And on the contrary, what commodities are brought home in exchange, they sell at what unreasonable rates they please, the whole commodity remaining in their hands; whereby the people in general, are very much damnified, and the companies only enriched; whereas, if the trade were free, our own commodities, having more chapmen, would sell at better rates, and what is brought home in return, would be distributed at much cheaper prices amongst the people.

This is for the most part a truth, yet, rightly considering the thing, it rather seems an advantage in the whole, than the least prejudice; for indeed, as they make their profit at home, so they make no less advantage abroad; for the whole commodity being in their hands, they will make the most that can be made of it; none having the like commodities to undersell them; and the like advantage they have again in what they buy; whereby in truth, our own commodities are sold the dearer to strangers, and foreign commodities bought much the cheaper; when both would happen contrary in a free trade; where each will undersell the other, to vent most; and also purchase at any rates, to prevent the rest: besides, many times the trade is wholly lost, particulars being often too weak to maintain and undergo it, and there is nothing less of a commodity vented by a Company, than by single persons; for they will always furnish, as much as the trade requires; the more they vent, the more being their profit. Whereby it may appear, that companies both vent our own commodities to the best advantages and buy cheapest what we want from strangers; and the prejudice that may happen by them to the workmen, or home-chapmen, is fully recompensed by the clear profit they return to the public, of which they are members, as well as others. But if their particular profits be thought too great, it may be something moderated by a free liberty, that every one that please may be admitted of the Company on fit and reasonable terms.

England's Interest and Improvement (1663), 1673, in J.R. McCulloch, *Early English Tracts on Commerce*, 1952, pp. 218–19, 231, 234–7, 244–5.

50 Roger Coke, 1670

Preface to the Reader

The excellency of trade. And this is so well understood, that trade is now become the lady, which in this present age is more courted and celebrated than in any former by all the princes and potentates of the world, and that deservedly too; for she acquires not her dominion by the horrid and rueful face of war, whose footsteps leave ever behind them deep impressions of misery, devastation, and poverty, but with the pleasant aspect of wealth and plenty of all things conducing to the benefit of human life and society, accompanied with strength to defend her, in case any shall attempt to ravish or invade her.

Epilogue

Thus, Reader, thou mayest understand, that though England be the most excellent and convenient place for trade of all others, yet our practice and ordering it is contrary to the nature of it; which ever flourishes most in convenient places, where it is more free, and people more abound. The abundance of our people (besides those which the hand of God hath taken away) are diminished in peopling our plantations, and in re-peopling Ireland since the late war and massacre there; so as thereby the strength as well as trade of the nation is abated proportionably; and yet as matters stand, we have interrupted our trade with Ireland. Nor can we for the future expect any great benefit from the trade to our plantations for tobaccos and sugars. For the Dutch by the late Treaty at Breda being possessed of Surinam, which yields better sugars than our Barbadoes, and may do in a much more inexhaustible manner, being upon the continent, and as good tobaccos as our Virginia; and being better masters of trade than we are, and having no laws of naturalization to restrain them from peopling it, and supplying themselves at home; we for the future can expect little other comfort from our plantations than to supply ourselves with sugars and tobaccos, but must leave the Dutch to enrich themselves with supplying the world thereby. . . .

As Ireland and our plantations have exhausted our men, whereby our trade and strength is abated and diminished, so the law against naturalization debars any future supply of other men from planting with us; and the law of navigation excludes much the greater trading part of the world from trading with us from abroad, and our corporations restrain our trade to as few at home; so as trade, which ever flourishes in multitude and freedom, is by us, by all imaginable ways, circumscribed, taxed, and reduced to a few.

While we are contriving newer and more severe laws against the exportation of wool, and neglect the careful inspection and management of our woollen manufactures, whereby they have lost their reputation abroad; we put the world upon necessities of supplying themselves elsewhere, and especially from Ireland: whereby the Dutch not only partake with us in our Turkey trade, and up the Elbe, but the Dutch and French in our own markets in England have a free and open trade in woollen cloths and stuffs; and in the meanwhile our wool becomes a drug, and of no price or esteem at home: whereby, notwithstanding the severity of all our laws against the exportation thereof, great quantities are exported; and so will be until we establish such a trade in our woollen manufactures, that men shall be better encouraged to work them here than elsewhere; for all men will rather venture their lives than lose their means of living.

We neglect to give any encouragement in assisting ingenuous and industrious men in any undertaking for the public good. I give one instance in the county of Suffolk, and here in Clerkenwell: the English during the late Dutch and French War did betake themselves to weaving poldavies, or buck, which they did make into double buck, being two threads spun together, and made of our

English hemp, (which Ipswich and Woodbridge men affirm to be better than any East Country hemp for this use) which made better sails than any other, and did manage a considerable trade thereby, to the great benefit of Suffolk: but now the Dutch and French buck is sold somewhat cheaper (the English not being as yet so much masters of the trade as the Dutch and French.) This trade begins to decline again, and to be neglected for want of some small encouragement, which might be done by some small imposition for some time upon the French and Dutch buck, until we should be enabled to work it as cheap, as it is in France and Holland.

As we give no encouragement to our industrious natives, so we utterly discourage all industrious foreigners from improving and increasing trade....

And the French King so well understands how much it will conduce to the advantage of France to encourage the freedom of trade, by entertaining all sorts of foreign artificers, that in contradiction to all the ecclesiastical powers opposing it, he hath granted free liberty to all sorts of foreign artificers and merchants to exercise their consciences in all ports and places in his dominion, and to have churches allowed them with equal or more privileges than his natural subjects. Sure now it will be no ways prudent in us so to discourage any herein, as to be entertained by the French King, as well as Dutch.

A Discourse of Trade, 1670, Preface, pp. 43–7.

51   Carew Reynel, 1674

We are come to this improvement that we are not so much by the indulgent care of rich men as by the wants of some ingenious persons forcing them to improve themselves for a livelihood. But what perfection should we arrive to if (in imitation of His Majesty and Royal Highness, who much encourage trade, ingenuity, and discoveries, even beyond any former princes) other great and rich persons would set about the work and private persons would get public spirits to labour after things so beneficial not only to the nation in general but to every man in particular. We take up our time about little businesses and it may be factious discourses when the whole profit of the nation, which is properly a nation of trade, lies unregarded. And half the charges that were spent in the last rebellion would have brought the gold of Guinea and riches of the Indies to us. . . .

As it is an advantage to have variety of manufactures, so also it is to have variety of husbandries, for the more several husbandries the ground is taken up with, the more every grain and commodity will vent one for another, and so advance the rate of land, produce greater profit and increase and maintain more people; but of all plantations at present, vineyards, orchards for cider, and tobacco plantations would be the most advantageous, especially tobacco; it sets an infinite [*sic*] of people on work, increaseth the rent of land, and returns great profit to the planter as can be proved beyond all exceptions, if time and occasion required.

The True English Interest, 1674, Preface and p. 19.

52 Anon, 1680

It does much import all English gentlemen, owners of land, and others, who take themselves to be sharers in the national interest, to examine the past and present state of our trade, and to seek for a legal regulation of it; and that all private interests destructive to our trade ought to be relaxed, and given up for the future.

Private interest is that many-headed monster, I am chiefly to encounter with, in which if any particular person shall take himself to be concerned, I shall desire him to consider, whether his own condition would not be more truly honourable and safe under more open methods of trade? I shall pray him to look into the nature of mere private interest, which, if he do, he must confess it the same principle that leads men into cheats, thefts, and all those other base, merciless and execrable villanies, which render the actors criminous, and odious by the sufferings and injuries they bring upon others.

Then if any man's particular way of gain be so prejudicial to trade, as to occasion the continual beggary of thousands of his countrymen, is not this more than equally mischievous to so many thousand thefts? But what if this beggary must unavoidably cause many thousand actual thefts, nay murders and enormities of all kinds, and as it grows more universal, must bring the nation into an impotent and indefensible weakness? Have we any amongst us that will be yet tenacious of such ways of gain? Will they tell us that they are not punishable by any laws in force? 'tis pity they are not. So there was a time when in old Rome, there was no direct law against parricide: but that they may no longer shelter themselves under this umbrage, it were highly necessary that laws were made to control them, and to remove all obstructions in our trade.

That trade is of this national importance and influence, and that the trade of England, in particular, hath been and continues under these disadvantages, will, I think, sufficiently appear to any indifferent reader, by the following discourse.

Britannia Languens, or a Discourse of Trade (1680), in McCulloch, *Early English Tracts on Commerce*, 1952, pp. 287–8.

53 Adam Smith, 1776

Though the encouragement of exportation, and the discouragement of importation, are the two great engines by which the mercantile system proposes to enrich every country, yet with regard to some particular commodities, it seems to follow an opposite plan: to discourage exportation and to encourage importation. Its ultimate object, however, it pretends, is always the same, to enrich the country by an advantageous balance of trade. It discourages the exportation of the materials of manufacture, and of the instruments of trade, in order to give our own workmen an advantage, and to enable them to undersell those of other nations in all foreign markets: and by restraining, in this manner, the exportation of a few commodities, of no great price, it proposes to occasion a much greater and more valuable exportation of others. It encourages the importation of the materials of manufacture, in order that our own people may be enabled to work them up more cheaply, and thereby prevent a greater and more valuable importation of the manufactured commodities. I do not observe, at least in our Statute Book, any encouragement given to the importation of the instruments of trade. When manufactures have advanced to a certain pitch of greatness, the fabrication of the instruments of trade becomes itself the object of a great number of very important manufactures. To give any particular encouragement to the importation of such instruments, would interfere too much with the interest of those manufactures. Such importation, therefore, instead of being encouraged, has frequently been prohibited. . . .

The importation of the materials of manufacture has sometimes been encouraged by an exemption from the duties to which other goods are subject, and sometimes by bounties. . . . The private interest of our merchants and manufacturers may, perhaps, have extorted from the legislature these exemptions, as well as the greater part of our other commercial regulations. They are, however, perfectly just and reasonable, and if, consistently with the necessities of the state, they could be extended to all the other materials of manufacture, the public would certainly be a gainer.

The avidity of our great manufacturers, however, has in some cases extended these exemptions a good deal beyond what can justly be considered as the rude materials of their work. By the 24 Geo. II. chap. 46. a small duty of only one penny the pound was imposed upon the importation of foreign brown linen yarn, instead of much higher duties to which it had been subjected before, viz. of sixpence the pound upon sail yarn, of one shilling the pound upon all French and Dutch yarn, and of two pounds thirteen shillings and fourpence upon the hundred weight of all spruce or Muscovia yarn. But our manufacturers were not long satisfied with this reduction. By the 29th of the same king, chap. 15, the same law which gave a bounty upon the exportation of British and Irish linen of which the price did not exceed eighteen pence the yard, even this small duty upon the importation of brown linen yarn was taken away. In the different operations, however, which are necessary for the preparation of linen yarn, a good deal more industry is employed, than in the subsequent operation of preparing linen cloth from linen yarn. To say nothing of the industry of the flax-growers and flax-dressers, three or four spinners, at least, are necessary, in order to keep one weaver in constant employment; and more than four-fifths of the whole quantity of labour, necessary for the preparation of linen cloth, is employed in that of linen yarn; but our spinners are poor people, women commonly, scattered about in all different parts of the country, without support or protection. It is not by the sale of their work, but by that of the complete work of the weavers, that our great master manufacturers make their profits. As it is their interest to sell the complete manufacture as dear, so is it to buy the materials as cheap as possible. By extorting from the legislature bounties upon the exportation of their own linen, high duties upon the importation of all foreign linen, and a total prohibition of the home consumption of some sorts of French linen, they endeavour to sell their own goods as dear as possible. By encouraging the importation of foreign linen yarn, and thereby bringing it into competition with that which is made by our own people, they endeavour to buy the work of the poor spinners as cheap as possible. They are as intent to keep down the wages of their own weavers, as the earnings of the poor spinners, and it is by no means for the benefit of the workman, that they endeavour either to raise the price of the complete work, or to lower that of the rude materials. It is the industry which is carried on for the benefit of the rich and the powerful, that is principally encouraged by our mercantile system. That which is carried on for the benefit of the poor and the indigent, is too often, either neglected, or oppressed....

The exportation of the materials of manufacture is sometimes discouraged by absolute prohibitions, and sometimes by high duties.

Our woollen manufacturers have been more successful than any other class of workmen, in persuading the legislature that the prosperity of the nation depended upon the success and extension of their particular business. They have not only obtained a mono-poly against the consumers by an absolute prohibition of importing woollen cloths from any foreign country; but they have likewise obtained another monopoly against the sheep farmers and growers of wool, by a similar prohibition of the exportation of live sheep and wool. The severity of many of the laws which have been enacted for the security of the revenue is very justly complained of, as imposing heavy penalties upon actions which, antecedent to the statutes that declared them to be crimes, had always been under-stood to be innocent. But the cruellest of our revenue laws, I will venture to affirm, are mild and gentle, in comparison of some of those which the clamour of our merchants and manufacturers has extorted from the legislature, for the support of their own absurd and oppressive monopolies. Like the laws of Draco, these laws may be said to be all written in blood. . . .

It has been shown in the foregoing part of this work, that the effect of these regulations has been to depress the price of English wool, not only below what it naturally would be in the present times, but very much below what it actually was in the time of Edward III. The price of Scots wool, when in consequence of the union it became subject to the same regulations, is said to have fallen about one half. It is observed by the very accurate and intelligent author of the *Memoirs of Wool*, the Reverend Mr John Smith, that the price of the best English wool in England is generally below what wool of a very inferior quality commonly sells for in the market of Amsterdam. To depress the price of this commodity below what may be called its natural and proper price, was the avowed purpose of those regulations; and there seems to be no doubt of their having produced the effect that was expected from them. . . .

[The effect of this reduction in wool price] upon the quantity of the annual produce may not have been very considerable [but] its effect upon the quality, it may perhaps be thought, must necessarily have been very great. The degradation in the quality of English wool, if not below what it was in former times, yet below what it naturally would have been in the present state of improvement and cultivation, must have been, it may perhaps be supposed, very nearly in proportion to the degradation of price. As the quality depends upon the breed, upon the pasture, and upon the management and cleanliness of the sheep, during the whole progress of the growth of the fleece, the attention to these circumstances, it may naturally enough be imagined, can never be greater than in proportion to the recompense which the price of the fleece is likely to make for the labour and expense which that attention requires. It happens, however, that the goodness of the fleece depends, in a great measure, upon the health, growth, and bulk of the animal; the same attention which is necessary for the improvement of the carcase, is, in some respects, sufficient for that of the fleece. Notwithstanding the degradation of price, English wool is said to have been improved considerably during the course even of the present century. The improvement might perhaps have been greater if the price had been better; but the lowness of price, though it may have obstructed, yet certainly it has not altogether prevented that improvement.

The violence of these regulations, therefore, seems to have affected neither the quantity nor the quality of the annual produce of wool so much as it might have been expected to do (though I think it probable that it may have affected the latter a good deal more than the former); and the interest of the growers of wool, though it must have been hurt in some degree, seems, upon the whole, to have been much less hurt than could well have been imagined.

These considerations, however, will not justify the absolute prohibition of the exportation of wool. But they will fully justify the imposition of a considerable tax upon that exportation.

To hurt in any degree the interest of any one order of citizens, for no other purpose but to promote that of some other, is evidently contrary to that justice and equality of treatment which the sovereign owes to all the different orders of his subjects. But the prohibition certainly hurts, in some degree, the interest of the growers of wool, for no other purpose but to promote that of the manufacturers....

The laudable motive of all these regulations, is to extend our own manufactures, not by their own improvement, but by the depression of those of all our neighbours, and by putting an end, as much as possible, to the troublesome competition of such odious and disagreeable rivals. Our master manufacturers think it reasonable, that they themselves should have the monopoly of the ingenuity of all their countrymen. Though by restraining, in some trades, the number of apprentices which can be employed at one time, and by imposing the necessity of a long apprenticeship in all trades, they endeavour, all of them, to confine the knowledge of their respective employments to as small a number as possible; they are unwilling, however, that any part of this small number should go abroad to instruct foreigners.

Consumption is the sole end and purpose of all production; and the interest of the producer ought to be attended to, only so far as it may be necessary for promoting that of the consumer. The maxim is so perfectly self-evident, that it would be absurd to attempt to prove it. But in the mercantile system, the interest of the consumer is almost constantly sacrificed to that of the producer; and it seems to consider production, and not consumption, as the ultimate end and object of all industry and commerce.

In the restraints upon the importation of all foreign commodities which can come into competition with those of our own growth, or manufacture, the interest of the home-consumer is evidently sacrificed to that of the producer. It is altogether for the benefit of the latter, that the former is obliged to pay that enhancement of price which this monopoly almost always occasions.

It is altogether for the benefit of the producer that bounties are granted upon the exportation of some of his productions. The home-consumer is obliged to pay, first, the tax which is necessary for paying the bounty, and secondly, the still greater tax which necessarily arises from the enhancement of the price of the commodity in the home market....

It cannot be very difficult to determine who have been the contrivers of this whole mercantile system; not the consumers, we may believe, whose interest has been entirely neglected; but the producers, whose interest has been so carefully attended to; and among this latter class our merchants and manufacturers have been by far the principal architects. In the mercantile regulations, which have been taken notice of in this chapter, the interest of our manufacturers has been most peculiarly attended to; and the interest, not so much of the consumers, as that of some other sets of producers, has been sacrificed to it.

The Wealth of Nations ed. Edwin Cannan, Methuen, 1961, II, pp. 159–61, 164–5, 169–72, 179–81.

Mercantilist Theory after 1660 and its Sources of Inspiration

54   Sir Josiah Child, 1669

The trade of England not decayed in gross but increased. To consider how the Dutch have advanced their trade. The Dutch are very faithful in the seal. Aulnage was intended an advantage but now the tickets are to be bought. There wants a regulation upon our fish. None will give credit to the packing of them. They give encouragement to all inventors. Here a patent is granted, there the party rewarded, and the design made public. Their ships are of small burden and useful. Their thrifty way of living. The education of their children. The lowness of their custom. The well-providing for their poor and employing of them. He conceives the laws not good because the parishes provide for themselves only. Their banks and Lombards. Their law merchant very useful. The way to promote trade is to increase the stock of the nation. To make returns of commodities by bills of exchange. To upon [*sic*] which traffic is now current. Registers useful. The frugality in all their public affairs. Their easy admission of burghers. Their multitude of navigable rivers. The lowness of their interest. The increase of the fishing trade. The freedom makes the nation valiant. All men are led by ease or profit. They have gotten all trade from us but what is ours by fortification natural or artificial. They can have no trade of our pilchards because they might be saved of our shore. Newfoundland fish. New plantations. In cloth, if they could, the 3 per cent would root us out of all. Liberty of religion. Trading people are musing people. The persecution of other places brought us our· divers trades, Milan fustians and jean fustians. Comfit making brought in by one that escaped the Inquisition. Trade of Maidstone thread carried all the world over. Silk-throwing and silk dyeing maintains 20,000 people in this city. Post office by Burlamachi. Statute bankrupt prejudicial to trade. All taxes that lay impositions upon our own commodities prejudicial to trade. Advantage of trade would have all freedom laid open. The statute of 5 Eliz. against exercising a trade without serving apprenticeship prejudicial. The exportation of coin hurtful. Bylaws among artificers very destructive. The want of hands is one cause of decay of trade. The fire in London and the plague. The great land taxes not preceded these judgements. The usual plenty of corn. The racking up of rents '51 and '52. The great improvement of Ireland. The Irish Act well intended but hath not taken the effect. They now send the beef into the plantations. An Englishman can hardly put in a ship into any Irish port being stopped up by the Dutch. The late innovated trade by the bankers in London. While interest goes up, land must go down. Anticipation of His Majesty's revenue. Our fishing trade in Newfoundland very small. Our cloth trade hath not increased here by the great increase of it in Germany and in other countries. New tax upon cloth in France. The Eastland and Norway trade much impaired. All Easterlings have liberty of bringing any trade hither. There is in the charges nothing to balance the account but a small impost to balance the profit. Nothing to remedy this but to lay a considerable tax upon the ships. If the French king take exception, he hath laid the like upon us. Another cause of the decay of the Eastland trade, the straitness of the trade; they admit none unless they give 20*li.* The Russia Greenland Company. They have lost the Greenland trade and now call for help. We had but one ship this year and the Dutch 3 or 400. Two ways only appear for the cure of the Irish trade: that they bring what they can of the native commodity but no foreign. The Scotch trade quite lost to the English by laying high duties on both sides. Whatever tends to the increase of hands and stocks doth increase the trade of a nation. Taking off burdens makes trades easy. The way to make it necessary. Usurers must let the money lie dead or purchase lands. Industry more profitable than idleness. All trade a kind of warfare.

Notes of the Lords' Committee on the Decay of Rents and Trade, 1669, in Joan Thirsk and J.P. Cooper, eds, *Seventeenth-Century Economic Documents,* Clarendon Press, 1972, pp. 69–70.

55   W. Letwin, 1963

Index of sources for Child's list of Dutch practices

Child's List	Robinson[1]	Worsley[2]	Lambe[3]	Dutch[4]
1. Merchants council	p. 5,No.16 Cf. p. 46	p. 9, No.4	p. 7,No.1	
2. Gavelkind		p. 10,No.3A	p. 8,No.2	
3. Exact making	p. 4, No.6	p. 7, No.3	p. 8,No.3	
4. Inventors	p. 4, No.7 Cf. p. 18	p. 10,No. 6	p. 9,No.5	
5. Shipping		p. 3,No. 1		p. 52, No.1
6. Parsimony				p. 53, No.5 Cf. pp. 56–7
7. Education of children				p. 55
8. Taxes[5]	p. 4,No.3 Cf. p. 9	p. 9,No.5	p. 8,No.4	
9. Poor	p. 4,No. 4			pp. 55–6
10. Banks	p. 4,No.11	p. 10,No.2A	p. 9,No.6	
11. Toleration				pp. 48–9
12. Law merchant	p. 4,No.10		p. 13; PS, p. 3	
13. Bills of debt	p. 5,No.12		pp. 12–13?	
14. Register of titles	p. 36			
15. Low interest	p. 4,No.2 Cf. p. 6	p. 10,No.1A		
Objections to lowering interest	pp. 7 ff.			

W. Letwin, *The Origins of Scientific Economics: English Economic Thought, 1660–1776*, Methuen, 1963, p. 240.

[1] Henry Robinson, *England's Safety, in Trades Encrease* (1641; Kress, 597).
[2] [Benjamin Worsley], 'Philopatris', *The Advocate* (1651; Kress, 837).

³ Samuel Lambe, *Seasonable Observations*...(1657; Kress, S. 429).
⁴ *The Dutch Drawn to Life* (1664; Kress, 1133).
⁵ In addition to other sources, see [William Petty], *Treatise on Taxes and Contributions* (1662; Kress, 1098; 1667 ed.), 35, 72, and *passim*.

Economic Development

56 Anon, 1675

It is but half an age or in fresh memory since improvements in husbandry began to have any name or to bear any credit in England. Sir Hugh Plat had a long and tedious task and spent many years in pleas, defences, apologies, solicitations, printing and reprinting many tracts before the husbandry would stir. But by importunities and perseverance at last he prevailed so far that in most counties they were convinced, and began to see and taste and enjoy the public benefit. And after our dismal wars broke out, in the intervals some were by necessity constrained to seek out all advantages they could hear of. . .and thus on a sudden the humour and spirit of a people is altered. Books of husbandry are sold off as fast as the press can print them. . . . Of these Hartlib's *Legacy* and Sir Richard Weston's *Husbandry of Brabant* carried the greatest esteem and prevalency in these days, each of them soon coming abroad in a fourth edition with amendments and additions. By all which helps and improvements the soil and agriculture of England was very much enriched above what it was in the reign of Queen Elizabeth.

Philosophical Transactions of the Royal Society, x, no. 114, 1675, pp. 320–1.

57 John Houghton, 1682

Since His Majesty's most happy Restoration the whole land hath been fermented and stirred up by the profitable hints it hath received from the Royal Society, by which means parks have been disparked, commons enclosed, woods turned to arable, and pasture lands improved by clover, sainfoin, turnips, coleseed, purslane, and many other good husbandries, so that the food of cattle is increased as fast, if not faster, than the consumption, and by these means, although some particular lands may fall, I strongly persuade myself that altogether the rent of the kingdom is far greater than ever it was.

A Collection of Letters for the Improvement of Husbandry and Trade, ed. Richard Bradley, 1728, IV, p. 85.

58   Richard Baxter, 1696

Gentlemen (mistake me not) the sum of my request to you is but this, that you will regard the public welfare of the nation above any few particular cases, and the interest of Christian religion in the souls of men above all your worldly interest and fleshly pleasure, and that you will, on such accounts, set your lands to the poorer sort of your tenants at such rates as by their labour and frugality they may comfortably live on, so as not to be necessitated by care for their rents, and by tiresome excess of labour, to be strangers to God's word, and to forbear family religion and to be prayerless or sleep when they should pray, and to live in ignorance for want of good books or time to read them, and think of what they hear at church; and that poverty constrain them not to educate their children like themselves. This [is] all that I have now to request of you.

In order to this, I think it would be a blessed example to the nation, if to such poor tenants you would abate a third part of your rack rents. (Some great ones that know where I was born, may know what I instance in.) When most tenants fifty years ago sat on the old rents, perhaps some one landlord set his land on the rack rent from year to year, and was hardly spoken of for it by all the country. If another come and buy his land and then raise it higher and set that at £50 or £60 which he set at £40, and that at £40 which he set at £30, and that at £4 which he set at £2 or £3, may not I justly petition that the poor people may have the clemency of their former rack which they called *cruelty?* This is no rare case. Few scruple raising rents to as much as they can get, when poor men, rather than beg and have no dwelling, will promise more than they can pay; and then, with care and toil, make shift as long as they can; and then run away and do so in another country. And so the gentlemen lose more by their *racking* than they get, whereas if they would abate a third part, and let their tenants live a comfortable life, they might have their rents constantly paid, and have the people's love, and partake of the comforts of those that are benefited or comforted by them.

To this end I humbly entreat you, gentlemen, to retrench your needless and sinful charges for superfluities, prodigality, and fleshly lust. That you may not need so much to feed your sin as will not leave you enough to discharge your duty to God and to the poor. Cannot you live as healthfully and decently with fewer dishes, and less variety, and less cost and curiosity, and less ostentation, attendance and pomp? Do not your tables and your furniture speak unbelief and contempt of Christ?

The Reverend Richard Baxter's Last Treatise, ed. F.J. Powicke, Manchester University Press, 1926, pp. 38–9.

Economic Continuity or Discontinuity?

59   E. Lipson, 1931

In the Age of Mercantilism the issue was fought out whether individualism should be allowed a free hand or kept rigorously under control, whether the dissolving forces of commercialism should ruthlessly destroy the mediaeval fabric of society or remain subject to the traditional checks and balances. The issue was a momentous one for the future destiny of the English people. The old order had judged economic conduct by an ethical standard which took account of its social reactions: the new order judged economic conduct by the standard of enlightened self-interest. The ideal of the old order was stability: that of the new order was progress. For a century (1558–1660) England was distracted by the conflict between these rival concepts. It is not, perhaps, the province of the historian to consider whether she would have been a happier country if she had retained some, at least, of the fetters which clogged individualism: wisely or unwisely she sacrificed them on the altar of progress. The 'Industrial Revolution' was not the cause of the triumph of the entrepreneur—on the contrary, it came first to England because the entrepreneur had already been liberated from the prison-house of tradition and authority....

In this enumeration of the reasons for the failure of the monarchy, we reach the final consideration. Even if the Crown had been supported by a staff of trained administrators, it could not have averted, though it might have modified, the establishment of a capitalist society. For while it was fortified by the prestige of centuries and by the innate loyalty and conservatism of the English people, it was impotent to check the insidious advance of individualism. Alike in industry, commerce and agriculture the foundations of the old order had been sapped by the subtle penetration of the spirit of capitalism. The mediaeval fabric still retained much of its old aspect, but its vitality had been largely drained away until there often remained little more than an empty shell. However, the struggle between the monarchy and the middle class might have proved more protracted and the issue might have continued longer in suspense but for the outbreak of the Civil War. The revolt against authority in the constitutional and religious spheres swept away the obstacles which had hitherto stifled the protests against authority in the economic sphere. The dissolution of the bonds which held society together had abiding consequences. A violent shock was given to institutions which had regulated the workings of the economic system, and although the process of change had begun, it was immensely accelerated by the decay of the legal sanctions. When a settled government was at length established, it was unable to revive in their fullness the authoritarian traditions which had enabled the monarchy to destroy or penalize enclosures; to bring pressure to bear on employers; to require local magistrates to provide work for the poor; to insist on technical training for artisans; to assess wages; to place individuals or corporations in charge of a branch of industry; and in other ways to superintend the economic life of the community. As the outcome of the Great Rebellion the movement towards *laissez-faire* acquired increasing momentum. In the relaxation of State control lies the economic significance of the Civil War.

After the Restoration, more than a century before the 'Industrial Revolution' or the publication of *The Wealth of Nations*, the doctrine of economic freedom began to gain an increasing hold over the minds of the governing body. A number of factors were working in this direction. In the first place, the development of capitalism and the stimulus of expanding trade had fostered and brought to maturity the nascent individualism of the middle class: already released from the jurisdiction of the craft gilds, it was grown ripe for the assertion of industrial liberty against the State itself.... In the second place, the new political system, which now prevailed, favoured economic emancipation since the monarchy could no longer exercise a restraining influence. The collapse of the authoritarian regime proved to be the turning-point in the evolution of capitalism in England. It eliminated the one barrier which obstructed the path of the entrepreneur who was allowed henceforth a freer hand in industry. The constitutional order established at the Restoration and consolidated by the Revolution of 1688 created the framework within which a capitalist society could work out its destiny unhampered by the control which the Crown had endeavoured to enforce. If the constitutional changes were themselves mainly the result of the growth of the middle class, they in turn stimulated its political instincts and commercial progress. Voltaire penetratingly observed that 'as trade enriched the citizens in London, so it contributed to their freedom; and this freedom on the other side extended their commerce'.[1] In the third place, the Civil War proved a powerful dissolvent of traditional ways of thought. The reaction against constituted authority extended inevitably to the economic field, and encouraged a critical attitude towards State interference. The vigorous attack made by a group of Restoration writers upon restraints in internal trade and industry revealed the extent to which a growing body of public opinion had emancipated itself from many of the dogmas enshrined in the outlook of the age. In the fourth place, the trend of the judicial decisions given in courts of law was in favour of industrial freedom, and the judges were particularly potent in circumscribing the scope of the Statute of Apprentices and in undermining the legal position of the craft guilds. In the fifth place, the waning power of the Privy Council—whose multifarious activities, mirrored in its records, had pervaded every branch of the national economy— weakened irreparably the existing mechanism of administration. Once the Government ceased to wield its former authority, the structure of which it had been the pivot began to disintegrate, and the economic functions of the local bodies in consequence largely lapsed.

The combined weight of all these factors produced an orientation of policy, which found expression in a definite advance towards *laissez-faire*. Owing to the movement which culminated in the Revolution of 1688, Parliament came directly under the influence of a capitalist regime which had successfully challenged the right of the Crown to limit its power, and proceeded to demand its liberation from the shackles laid upon it by the legislature. Nothing was to be allowed to stand in the path of the entrepreneur: even the case for religious toleration was based on the plea that persecution was a bar to prosperity in view of the prominence of the

[1] Voltaire, *Letters concerning the English Nation,* (1733 edn.) p. 69.

Dissenters in the business world. Henceforth Parliament concentrated its energies upon commercial policy, which was now systematically designed to protect the interests of the producer and ensure him the undisputed possession of the home market: it grew less concerned to control industry, regulate labour conditions, and promote social stability. In accordance with the change of attitude, the old industrial code was allowed gradually to fall into desuetude. The whole economic outlook of the eighteenth century was permeated by an encroaching individualism which insisted upon unfettered freedom of action, and imposed upon the Government the course that it must pursue. Owing to this reversal of roles, the State renounced the right to dictate to entrepreneurs the terms on which they should employ their workfolk, and exhibited an increasing disposition to tolerate their claims to make their own contract regarding the rates of remuneration, the length of service, the quality and supply of labour, and the nature of the products. Parliament pronounced the maxim in 1702 which was to mould its policy throughout the century—'Trade ought to be free and not restrained'.

The Economic History of England, II: The Age of Mercantilism, A. and C. Black, 1956 edn, pp. cxv-cxvi, cxxiv-cxxviii.

60   Christopher Hill, 1961

Economics, 1640–60

Employers and *entrepreneurs* were freed from government regulation and control in various ways. Attempts to supervise quality of manufactures and to fix prices were abandoned; industrial monopolies were abolished. Greater freedom was established in relations between employers and workmen. The government stopped trying to regulate wage rates, to compel employers to keep their employees at work in time of slump. Taxation became regular, if heavy, and (except under Army rule) it was controlled by representatives of the taxpayers. Henceforth employers were limited in expanding or contracting their business solely by economic considerations.

'The relation between masters and servants,' wrote Clarendon nostalgically, was 'dissolved by the Parliament, that their army might be increased by the prentices against their masters' consent.' The Act of 1563, insisting on a seven-year period of apprenticeship, and excluding all but freeholders' sons from apprenticeship, was not enforced. The common law, so favourable to absolute property rights, triumphed over the prerogative courts.

Economics, 1660–88

After 1660 the landowning class was secure against social revolt from below. Henceforth a major preoccupation of governments was to stimulate production and to protect the producer, no longer to safeguard the consumer or to protect the subsistence farmer. This marks a decisive change in outlook. Parliament did much to help the improving lessee, for example by authorizing the crown to enclose forest lands for cultivation. Regrating and engrossing (buying corn in the open market and storing it for re-sale when scarcity had raised prices) were permitted under an Act of 1663, whose object was to stimulate cultivation of waste land by giving 'sufficient encouragement... for the laying out of cost and labour'. By the end of the sixties corn import was virtually prohibited, so as to keep home prices high. From 1673 to 1681 bounties were granted on exported wheat—a 'revolution in our fiscal policy', Professor Hughes calls it. Bounties were discontinued during the period of personal government; they returned with the Liberator in 1689. Protection against imports, and this export bounty, steadied wheat prices and greatly reduced the speculative element in agriculture. Production was stimulated....

The post-Restoration atmosphere was conducive to capital investment and scientific experiment. The Royal Society made suggestions for agricultural improvement, 'by which means parks have been disparked, commons enclosed, woods turned into arable, and pasture lands improved by clover... so that the food of cattle is increased as fast if not faster than the consumption'. Racking of rents was justified because having to pay more to landlords encouraged tenants to work harder and to grow new crops. One argument in favour of fen drainage was that it not only rendered fresh land available for cultivation but also forced poor squatters to 'quit idleness and betake themselves to... manufactures', thus reducing unemployment. Fortrey argued in 1663 that 'as many or more families may be maintained and employed in the manufacture of the wool that may arise out of 100 acres of pasture, than can be employed in a far greater quantity of arable'. Industry could now absorb a greater proportion of those evicted; this helped to generate opinion favourable to enclosures.

. . . The Restoration saw no attempt to revive the authoritarian régime in industry. When in 1664 a Bill before Parliament proposed to revive the pin monopoly, at a meeting of wire-drawers one of them was heard to declare that the late King had lost his head for granting such patents. The Bill was allowed to drop; and it is significant of the decline in the royal prerogative that it was a Bill. Parliamentary statutes were now sovereign, and there was no Star Chamber to enforce monopolies.

The Cromwellian ordinance authorizing disbanded soldiers to practise trades to which they had not been apprenticed was re-enacted in 1660; the attitude of the now triumphant common-law courts ensured that restrictive gild and apprentice regulations were never again effectively enforced except in agriculture. An Act of 1663 threw the linen industry open to all. In 1669 a draper said of the Elizabethan Statute of Apprentices that 'though not repealed, yet [it] has been by most of the judges looked upon as inconvenient to trade and to the increase of inventions'. The Privy Council accepted his contention. In 1685 the courts ruled that apprenticeship was necessary only for servants hired by the year, thus exempting most wage labourers from it. In 1689, of 200 towns in England, only a quarter had any organised gilds at all. The prosperity of Birmingham and its industries in the later seventeenth century is attributed to the fact that it was not a chartered borough: it had no gilds, and its many dissenters were free from the restrictions imposed by the Clarendon Code. The clothing industry benefited especially from the new freedom. . . .

England, Fortrey thought in 1663, could support twice its population, 'were they rightly employed'. The problem was to find the right form of organization. It was assumed that the poor would work only to avoid starvation: this was one reason for encouraging corn export, in order to keep wheat prices high. Landlords benefited doubly, by high rents from prosperous farmers and easily obtained labour from people who had to work for dear life. One effect of the Restoration, indeed, was to strength-

en the position of the employing classes. 'We find the unreasonable-
ness of servants' [i.e. wage labourers'] wages a great grievance,'
said the Grand Jury (i.e. chief landowners) of Worcestershire in
1661; 'servants are grown so proud that the master cannot be
known from the servant.' In order to put the lower orders back
in their place, the Jury added, the authority of Justices of the
Peace should be enhanced.

The 1662 Act of Settlement, passed partly to solve the problem
set by masses of disbanded soldiers seeking work, authorized
Justices to send back to his last place of domicile any newcomer
to a parish who seemed likely to become a charge on the rates.
Thus only persons of some standing could move, even to look
for work, without the consent of the Justices. In Thorold Rogers's
words, the Settlement Act made the labourer 'a serf without land'.
The assumption behind the statute was that a pauper was idle,
vicious, and rightless. The impotent poor received relief in their
parish of settlement, at minimum rates. Workhouses were deliberately made unpleasant in order to discourage applicants for relief;
so they helped to keep down wages outside. This harsh code was
more effective in villages than in towns. Hence the drift to the
greater freedom and economic opportunity of the cities, where a
mass of casual labour prevented wages rising too rapidly and
began to form that new phenomenon, the mob.

We have little evidence of what the poor themselves thought.
The Restoration confirmed the defeat of democratic movements
in London. Before the end of the century the small masters in
most City companies had lost all influence in running their affairs;
everywhere oligarchy ruled. Industrial struggles began to take
more modern forms. There were strikes and mutinies in the
dockyards in the sixteen-sixties, and combinations to secure
higher wages.

Century of Revolution, Nelson, 1961, pp. 146, 202–7.

61   Charles Wilson, 1965

The economic regulations of the Interregnum were torn out of the
Statute Book along with the rest of its legislation. The early years

of the Restoration therefore saw a vigorous reconstruction of this apparatus of economic control and stimulation. Its principles were not new. Just as in earlier years, monarchical or republican, the aims remained those of economic and strategic self-sufficiency, expansion, and the exclusion of the Dutch from their dominant position in the economy. But the revived system was constructed by men with a greater skill and cunning that derived from longer and keener observation of the problems to be tackled, and with a shrewder awareness of the loopholes in the older legislation. Now, more than ever before, the legislator looked to the New World and Asia and Africa to seek freedom from the thraldom—as they saw it—to Dutch economic superiority in Europe.

Cloth no longer enjoyed quite its old and dangerous domination over exports: but it still remained far the largest manufacture, representing somewhere between three-quarters and a half of total exports by value. In September 1660, therefore, the King lent a ready ear to a petition from the clothiers. 'For some years past', they asserted, 'the Dutch have designed to beat down and discourage the manufacture in this realm, and to gaine the same to themselves, which they have in great measure effected...in order to that designe they have imposed immoderate imposts upon English cloth imported into their countries.' Demanding that such tariffs be revoked before any treaty was made with Holland they went on to ask for the old penalties against the export of wool, yarn, fuller's earth, etc., to be renewed, and the import of rival luxury textiles to be forbidden. Renewed they were; and the old regulations reserving the supply of local raw materials to this English industry were to be primed watchfully by successive administrations down to the Napoleonic wars.

The inadequacy of the Navigation Act of 1651 had become evident long before the Restoration. Even if the Act itself had not been repudiated it would have been necessary to amend it.... In the European trades, it had proved impossible to enforce the Act and even in the colonial trades it seemed to be more honoured in the breach than in the observance. The new Act of 1660 derived from the same principles and ambitions as its predecessors, but more effort was now directed to making its provisions workable, even if this meant limiting its objectives....

Was the System, as Adam Smith said, merely a conspiracy of merchants for their own interests, a plot which sacrificed the interests of consumers to those of producers, replacing 'one fruitless care' (the control of bullion) by another 'much more intricate, much more embarrassing, and equally fruitless' (the balance of trade)? How just was the charge that 'our merchants and manufacturers have been by far the principal architects'? And how did such charges square with the final concession that the Navigation Acts were 'perhaps the wisest of all the commercial regulations of England', which had properly sacrificed opulence to defence? More is known nowadays than was known to Adam Smith about the processes by which private and public interests were blended to issue in legislation. Economic reconstruction was the work of Crown and Parliament. But it was only part of the whole task of replacing disorder by order and this was plainly beyond the capacity of the twenty-eight members who comprised the Privy Council. An increased proportion of economic policy-making was therefore entrusted to committees of the Privy Council: the habit of inviting mercantile experts into consultation was an old and familiar one. Many of the same merchants and financiers who had advised Charles's father and even his grandfather, as well as many who had aided Cromwell, were now called in to help. Some were economic Vicars of Bray who had managed to serve all. Yet, except for the great bankers, they were rarely admitted into the innermost counsels of state. Commercial interests were consulted, M.P.s in Parliament and out urged the needs of regions and industries, brains were picked, knighthoods distributed, but the control of policy remained in the hands of the great politicians whose birthright government was. And 'policy' did not consist merely of satisfying the clamour of influential merchants or companies. It had to compass the preservation of public order that might be endangered by large-scale unemployment or food short-ages, the yield and collection of tax revenue, and problems of national defence. In the very early days, it did seem possible that two committees—those of Trade and of Foreign Plantations—might prove so heavily weighted by merchant members that the traditional machinery of government might be overwhelmed by sheer numbers. But like all overgrown committees they proved self-defeating. The interests of the members were too diverse to allow them any collective momentum. The conduct of day-to-day business reverted therefore to the great Companies. The Privy Councillors ceased to attend the swollen committees, and after declining into an academic debating society, the Council of Trade died of inanition in 1667. Over the Plantations Committee the Privy Council fairly swiftly re-established its hold. The habitual governing class who comprised it had the habit of command. Merchants had not.... Yet the grandees themselves could not manage the whole of public business and its intricate detail. They had their private business and pleasures to manage. They did not always have either the capacity or the application to endure protracted sessions of intricate discussion of public business, especially of economic affairs. This was doubtless the situation that Adam Smith had in mind when he wrote that between tradesmen who did not understand the principles of national policy and gentlemen who failed to grasp the principles of trade, policy fell into an erroneous obsession with trade balances. But he left out one element of supreme importance in policy-making: the presence of those Crown servants who, after the Restoration, and increasingly in the seventies and eighties, came to exercise a powerful influence on Crown policy. They sat in the Commons and on Privy Council committees, were to be found on the boards of the great Companies, and served in the great departments of state. In all these offices, men like the Coventrys (William and Henry), Sir George Downing, Sir Joseph Williamson, Sir Leoline Jenkins, and later, Sir William Blathwayt acted as interpreters and brokers between the interests of individuals and companies on the one hand, and the Government and the public interest (as they understood it) on the other....

What did this remarkable progress of trade and shipping owe to the system of legislation and control called, by a later and critical age, the mercantile system? Orthodox economists, following Adam Smith, were inclined to condemn it as by definition restrictive, monopolistic, mischievous or at least otiose. More recently, its central core—the Navigation Code—has had a better press. The most careful analysts have concluded that without its protection and stimulus, English trade and shipping would have found it difficult to develop against the greater skill, better technology and entrenched interests of the Dutch. Possibly some of these judgements, in their anxiety to do justice to the Acts, pay too little regard to those other elements of growth in the economy—to developing industries, the removal of internal regulations of medieval ancestry, to social mobility, the release and encouragement of enterprise, to sound government, naval power, natural endowment of material resources and perhaps a growing population. To isolate one chapter of legislation from its economic, social and political context and judge its effect is impossible. But it seems that the laws worked with, rather than against, the forward march of economic forces as a whole. They represented that growing investment of the nation's intelligence and enthusiasm in the cause of material gain. The results do not always bear an aspect pleasing to the liberal mind of a later age. Their logic was often the logic of power, physical force and war, and the increment of wealth did not seem as yet to percolate very far down society. Error, muddle and waste seemed often to be paramount. Yet though some contemporary minds might dissent from their application in particular cases (as the author of *Britannia Languens* or Dudley North did), few dissented from their principles. 'Armed aggression', a modern historian has said of this period, 'was the heart of commerce.'[1] Foreign contemporaries were inclined to think that the difference between the warmongering of the English and of the others was that the English wars represented a material objective broader than mere dynasticism, and one planned with a more cunning regard to the interests of His Majesty's subjects. They may have been right. . . .

Other economic changes sometimes attributed to the Civil War were often the continuance, in an intensified form, of phenomena already apparent long before the Civil War. The great Restoration Navigation Code itself (1660–63) represented a second, and more successful, attempt to codify the laws relating to shipping which Parliament had first tackled in 1651. Yet this in turn was foreshadowed in scores of earlier acts relating to shipping and especially in the attempt of 1622 to reserve the Baltic shipping trades to Englishmen. Indeed, the Restoration Government spent several busy years after the King's return re-enacting a whole catalogue of 'mercantilist' statutes relating to trade and industry. These included not only those which had been torn out of the Statute Book as disaffected and invalid but also revisions and extensions of early Stuart legislation such as the prohibitions against the export of wool, fuller's earth and other clothmaking materials. An administration strengthened by the accession of a new class of royal 'public' servants and more sensitive to the demands represented

[1] G.N. Clark, *The Seventeenth Century*, 2nd edn, 1947, p. 59.

by the restored Parliament was now moulding a revised set of formulae for economic policy. They had behind them the experience of the Interregnum as well as the period of personal government, and they legislated with an eye to the trade of the nation as a whole and not merely of London. The London companies, both chartered and joint stock, had been in rough waters between 1643 and 1660. Yet there was no clear-cut contrast between the attitudes of Kings and Protector to company organization. Charles had licensed rivals to the East India Company. Cromwell, in spite of the current prejudices against the old company, decided to retain it. The fortunes of a company after the Restoration depended broadly on its utility and its lobbying power. That the prejudices of the Interregnum did no permanent damage to the joint-stock image is shown by the Act of 1662 which protected stock holders in such companies by limiting their legal liability to the nominal value of their holding. The principle that monopoly might be justified in distant and difficult trades was thus confirmed: but the general enforcement of trade and maritime policy was transferred, under the Navigation Acts, from the companies to the State. After a brief period of ostentatious participation in commercial and colonial policy-making, the merchants gave way once more to the nobles and professional administrators. In traditional fashion, Government reaffirmed its right to govern.

While commercial policy was assuming more coherent patterns, manufactures seemed to be moving into a phase of freer growth and independence. How far was this the result of the Civil War and the dismantling of the Prerogative Courts and the whole central government machinery by which economic and social policy had been (at any rate theoretically) enforced under the early Stuarts? The answer must be: only partially and indirectly. Unlike the old urban crafts, the up and coming industries—textiles, metal working and mining—were not located in the narrow streets of the corporate town. They were dispersed widely over villages and countryside. 'Water power', Sir John Clapham wrote, 'had been a solvent of gild-power from the days of the first rural fulling mill.'[2] The increased industrial use of fuel and power continued its disintegration. Neither Manchester nor Birmingham nor any of the towns and villages where capital and markets for production were growing had gilds. Even in London the gilds were losing

[2] J. Clapham, *A Concise Economic History of Britain*, 1949, p. 253.

control over the workers of the sprawling suburbs. Likewise apprenticeship was in decline. Cromwell allowed demobilized soldiers into protected trades without apprenticeship. After the Great Fire the shortage of craftsmen dealt the system another blow. By the 1670s there were 'illegal' men in all occupations. All the economic forces of the day were pulling against these old forms of industrial regulation.

But this did not mean full or doctrinaire application of *laissez-faire*: nor did it necessarily mean the entirely heartless, anti-social regime described by some later historians. Wage-earners had not done well in the first half of the century. After 1650 they did a little better. The old system of wage assessment continued well into the eighteenth century. But on the whole the rise of wages seems to have come before the Justices gave it official recognition. The picture of a ruthlessly materialistic ruling class exploiting wage-earners and the poor is not borne out by the facts. That great severity and even brutality followed in the wake of e.g. the Settlement Laws of 1662 is undoubted. The power to eject immigrant paupers from a parish led to grievous hardship. But the preamble to the Act explains how these powers derived from the very measures taken by some parishes to deal with their own poor. Those parishes which most conscientiously did their duty 'were inundated by distressed paupers' from parishes which did not. The law, in fact, merely reflected the horrific proportions of the nation's major social problem between 1660 and 1834: the poor. There was no sudden change of ethos....

The permanent economic consequences of the Civil War and Interregnum owed little to any conscious or direct onslaught by one phalanx of economic interests on another. Such direct action as there was (against the great companies, for example) left little lasting impression. The effects were less direct and more subtle than that. They resulted from the abolition or reform of political and religious institutions undertaken principally for political and religious reasons. The end of the absolute monarchy, of the Prerogative Courts, and the new expanded role of Parliament created a matrix of government and law within which economic change and expansion could proceed with less anachronistic interference than under the old regime. Most if not all the economic trends observable in the century after 1660 were a continuation of earlier ones....

Many of the changes and improvements to be seen on English farms after the Restoration represented the natural extensions of earlier changes. The logic of enclosure was too strong to be resisted, and the attempts of Government and of social reformers, mostly abortive, to stop men enclosing by laws and by administrative action came to an end with the Restoration. The Privy Council, which had been the engine of Stuart social policy, now ceased to perform that function. The main executants of its policies, the prerogative Courts, had disappeared. Attempts at social planning had been an aspect of that idealism so characteristic of early Stuart government and so dangerous in execution, by turns desultory and severe. The more down-to-earth and cynical rulers of the century after the Restoration abandoned them as practically fruitless, economically backward, and politically inconvenient. Enclosure could now go forward, either by private Act of Parliament, or—more commonly—by the enrolment of the enclosure agreement in the Court of Chancery....

The bounty system did not inaugurate a Golden Age for the arable farmer. Prices from 1675 to 1700 were only poor to moderate, rising higher only in the 'barren years' of the nineties. Probably the bounty did no more than keep levels reasonably stable. The extension of new methods of arable farming in these years was therefore not a pursuit of easy profits but a means of adjusting arrangements so that a larger output at stable prices was obtained for the same or slightly larger costs.

If the bounty policy looks like another of those conspiracies between Government and the landed interest which has led some historians to suppose that government policy was wholly dictated by private interests, a glance at wool production suggests a different view. While the corn market might be the farmers' preserve, the wool market was reserved for the clothier. Here seventeenth-century policy consistently aimed at a bountiful supply of wool at low prices that helped the manufacturer to keep spinners and weavers busy, accepting it as axiomatic that it was uneconomic to export a primary material when it was possible to export it in a manufactured, and therefore more profitable, form. Scores of Acts prohibiting the export of wool testified to this belief, and it is fallacious to suppose they were of no effect....

Increased local, national production was the object also of the numerous Acts of Parliament and regulations made under them for stimulating, protecting and subsidizing other forms of trade and industry, including the cloth industry, and of the great Navigation Laws themselves. Later economists, of whom Adam Smith was the greatest, came to regard the whole system as a mischievous and corrupt distortion of the economy in the interests of private individuals. Such measures as comprised 'the mercantile system' constructed in these years subordinated 'consumption' to production and to the interests of producers, wrote Adam Smith. By Adam Smith's day, the criticisms of the system had some force, though they reflected, besides rational criticisms, some imagined and exaggerated ones. A century or so earlier, when the system was fashioned, it is arguable that it was the necessary matrix within which the infant economy had to be coaxed into growth. Of the economy as a whole, as of agriculture, the only incontrovertible fact is that it did improve and did grow. Trade, industry, agriculture, exports, ports, shipping all showed abundant evidence of vigour and enterprise in an age that lacked the convenient explanatory apparatus—spectacular price rises, population increase or revolutionary inventions—available in previous and subsequent periods of growth. While it may be conceded that the most obvious beneficiaries of the new policies *were* the 'producers'—landlords, farmers, manufacturers, merchants, shipowners—it can hardly be doubted that a rising volume of employment followed in the wake of their enterprise. Standards of living for the people at large might not yet show any spectacular or measurable rise, but certainly a larger population was living at standards that were not falling and were in some respects tending to improve. The expanding market for New Draperies, especially for the cheaper varieties like fustians, must have included a sizeable proportion of customers from the lower half of society. Even the luxuries of early Stuart times were now selling at prices poorer people could afford. Tobacco, which legend said was worth its weight in silver earlier in the century, could be had for $3\frac{1}{2}$d. a pound by 1680. The brewers were worried by the competition of coffee. Clothiers were feeling the effects of imported calicoes. And so on. Plainly, habits of consumption were changing, and not only among the rich. For all save the 'Poor'—and their numbers remained very large—life was a little more varied, a little less primitive.

England's Apprenticeship, 1603–1743, Longmans, 1965, pp. 161–3, 165–7, 184, 135–8, 236, 141, 148, 237–8.

62   Caroline Robbins, 1960

Continuities and successes at the Restoration are identical. These are the mercantilist policies of imperial development. The means of forwarding them already worked out now overrode all obstacles and reservations. The commercial spirit...chiefly moved the City and the General to seek the re-establishment of an order which promised greater stability. The new generation—Bennet, the Berkeleys, Ashley, Craven, Downing, and lesser but powerful folk like Povey and Noell—were absorbed by economic rather than political ambitions. Estates still 'made lords' and gentry. Privileges must be guarded, not a cony nor a bird be snared. Bounties and profits must be obtained from Parliament and King. The landed interest also sought wealth in trade and in colonial adventure, and their activities no doubt helped to satisfy some of the necessities of a growing population. In spite of Penn and his Quakers, this was a period of commercial rather than ideological colonization—a bustling, imperial, materialistic age. Many practical devices were extended and developed to expedite the expansion of the old empire—cabinet, committee, board, even party, all helped. The Cromwellian expedient of the union of the three kingdoms was dropped and the economic progress of Scotland set back a half-century. His Irish settlement was enforced by Navigation and Cattle Acts.

A mixture of mercantilism and free enterprise made England powerful and brought wealth to many.

'Fact and fancy in 1660', in *The Restoration of the Stuarts. Blessing or Disaster?*, Report of a Folger Library Conference, Folger Shakespear Library, 1960, pp. 39–40.

Part Five

THE RESTORATION OF THE SOCIAL ORDER

The Duke of Newcastle's advice to Charles II at the Restoration was that he should insist on ceremony and order, and draw firmer lines between the classes (63). This represented the hopes of a backward-looking Royalist, who wanted to restore the hierarchical class structure, which men had idealized, but utterly failed to sustain, even in the Elizabethan age. Few contemporaries were as outspoken as this; and yet events moved inexorably in this direction. A conservative reaction against the democratic tendencies of the Interregnum took hold, and as old families resumed their places in local government, as the gentry settled back in their manor houses and resumed their sway over parish life, and as merchants resumed their place on city councils, reluctance to disturb the power structure developed into torpor.

Many members of the old ruling class had known hard times during the Civil War and felt entitled to a few extravagances at the Restoration. Houghton (64) thought this no bad thing, for it goaded them into energetic improvement of their estates. But in achieving their social aspirations, the gentry pursued harsh economic policies which loosened further the ties of sympathy between themselves and the lower classes. Sir Ralph Verney's statement of his philosophy when letting land to tenants speaks volumes (65). He expressed his intentions in terms of economic justice: it was only fair that he should get an equitable rent. But in practice he fixed his rents as high as possible, higher than those paid on neighbouring estates, and evicted tenants when they fell in arrears for more than a year.* Thus the practical result of his

---

* I wish to thank Dr John Broad for drawing my attention to this document from the Verney archives, and for allowing me to give here the substance of Sir Ralph Verney's estate policy, which is fully elaborated in his unpublished thesis, 'Sir Ralph Verney and his Estates, 1630–96', Oxford University D. Phil. thesis, 1973, pp. 248, 195 ff.

philosophy was to save the fortunes of the Verney family, establish a few well-to-do tenant farmers on the estate, and slowly to cull out the smallholders.

The view among the upper classes that too much education had bred discontent in the lower ranks of society and had caused the civil war is presented here by the Duke of Newcastle (70), but it represented a widely held opinion. It helps to explain why educational opportunities dwindled in the later seventeenth century, and had the effect of further damping down social mobility, as Professor Stone demonstrates (71, 72).

Historians nowadays sum up social trends at the Restoration by focusing attention on the hardening core of gentry families in the counties, who also crept into positions of influence in the towns, thereby stiffening existing urban oligarchies (68). But it is important to remember that those gentlemen who survived the Restoration and were set fair for another hundred years were, in fact, in the upper ranks of their class. As H. J. Habakkuk argued in an article published in 1940 ('English landownership, 1680–1740'*), less stable conditions prevailed among the lower ranks. Smaller gentry often declined in fortune, along with many small freeholders. In some areas of the kingdom, notably in the lowland zone of England, tenant farms were reshaped to preserve a few large units and to eliminate small-holdings. A new middle class of substantial tenant farmers was established.

At the same time the professional class assumed greater economic and social importance. It drew its members mostly from among the younger sons of gentry and the educated middle class, having a taste for good living, and purses long enough to indulge that taste. They, and especially the lawyers, were the loyal allies of the entrenched landed gentry. The ruling class in local society was thus enlarged and consolidated. Professional men and prosperous merchants joined with the gentry in business, and exchanged marriage partners. By their acquisition of luxury goods and adornments, which they installed in their solidly comfortable houses, they conspicuously emphasized the distance that separated them from the poor. Some of their pleasures in food were bought at the direct expense of the common man (67).

*This influential article is not represented here as the author plans to revise it and bring it up-to-date in the light of more recent research. The original can be read in *Economic History Review*, x, 1940, pp. 2 ff.

Among urban craftsmen, traditionally organized in the gilds, the classes became more clearly differentiated, and fewer people were able to climb the social ladder from bottom to top. Power came to rest decisively in the hands of the wealthier craftsmen and merchants, while small masters sank into the ranks of workmen. Unwin (68) describes how the latter attempted to win the right to form their own combinations, but failed, and only secured it in the nineteenth century in trade unions.

That laissez-faire attitudes grew stronger and widened the gulf between rich and poor is made plain in the writing of the Puritan preacher, Richard Baxter (66). The decline of generosity and compassion was much lamented. Meanwhile, theoretical treatises on the social classes, written by churchmen, continued with the same assurance as before the revolution to justify the unequal division of wealth and to assign to each class its appropriate place in the hierarchy (73).

Social Order

63 The Duke of Newcastle, 1660

For Ceremony and Order

Ceremony, though it is nothing in itself, yet it doth everything.
For what is a king more than a subject but for ceremony and order?
When that fails him, he's ruined. What is the church without
ceremony and order? When that fails, the church is ruined. What
is the law without ceremony and order? When that fails, the law
goes down. What are the universities and all schools without
ceremony and order? Nothing. What are all corporations without
ceremony and order? Nothing. What is a lord more than a footman,
without ceremony and order? A despised title. What is parents
and children, masters and servants, officers in all kinds in the
Commonwealth without ceremony and order? Nothing at all.
Nay, what is an army without ceremony and order, and there the
strictest ceremony and order, for he that continues longest in
order, which is in bodies, wins the battle. What are all councils
and states without ceremony and order? Nothing but confusion
and ruin. So that ceremony and order, with force, governs all,
both in peace and war, and keeps every man and everything within
the circle of their own conditions. Nay, very bear baiting without
ceremony and order would be in more confusion than it is, and
many such like things. Therefore, your Majesty will be pleased
to keep it up strictly in your own person and court, to be a precedent
to the rest of your nobles and not to make yourself too cheap by
too much familiarity, which, as the proverb says, breeds contempt.
But when you appear to shew yourself gloriously to your people,
like a God—for the Holy Writ says, we have called you gods—
and when the people sees you thus, they will down of their knees,
which is worship and pray for you with trembling fear and love,

as they did to Queen Elizabeth, whose government is the best precedent for England's government absolutely, only these horrid times must make some little addition to set things straight, and so to keep them.... Certainly, there is nothing keeps up a king more than ceremony and order, which makes distance, and that brings respect and duty, and those obedience which is all. Nay, he is a fool that is too bold with your Majesty even in your bedchamber, and those that are so, I know your Majesty's wisdom will give them a check for it, and if they do not mend, put them out. And your Majesty will find much quiet and benefit by it.

So if your Majesty please to speak to your Heralds, to set down the ceremony and order for all degrees of your nobility, as for barons, viscounts, earls, marquises and dukes, and to have it printed, and so for all the great officers, their ceremony and order, and not any to entrench one upon another, but to keep only what is right and due for their places and dignities. It's one thing, none under the degree of a baroness can have carpets by her bed, and she but one or two at the most. And now every Turkey merchant's wife will have all her floor over with carpets. So now every citizen's wife will have six horses in her coach, which is most unfitting. They say the ways are so foul when 'tis their pride, for I am sure when I was a boy, Gilbert, the great Earl of Shrewsbury, never went but with four horses in his coach and those of meaner degrees but with two horses, and travelled many hundred miles, and the ways as foul as they are now. The king of Spain allows nobody six horses but himself. This your Majesty will rectify very easily. So to make no difference between great ladies and citizens' wives in apparel is abominable. No, they should go to their little black velvet caps, small gold chains, and little ruffs, as they were in my time, and their apprentices in their round black caps. But this must take a little time, for fear of offending too fast, until your Majesty be well settled in your saddle—and when any of these orders are violated, to be brought into your Marshall's court and there punished, which court, though it was spoken against in Parliament, is a most excellent court, for it keeps up ceremony and order, so the court be kept within his bounds—for certainly degrees of apparel to several conditions and callings is of great consequence to the peace of the kingdom, for when lower degrees strives to outbrave higher degrees, it breeds envy in the better sort, and pride in the meaner sort, and a contempt by the vulgar of the nobility, which breeds faction and disorder, which are the causes of a civil war.

Therefore, Sir, keep up your nobility and gentry to all their just rights and dignities. For what kept up your royal father so long but part of the nobility and gentry, when he had no money which was the sinews of war, maintaining themselves and his war almost at their own charge, and held out beyond all expectation? It was neither the church, nor the law that kept up the king so long, but part of the nobility and gentry. Therefore, your Majesty's wisdom will cherish them. 'Tis true wise kings heretofore took as much power from the nobility as they could because of the barons' wars, and put more to the Commons, wherein they committed a very great error. For the worst in the nobility is but to pull down one king, and set up another, so that they are always for monarchy. But the Commons pull down root and branch, and utterly destroys monarchy, so that your Majesty will be pleased to stick to your nobility and gentry. And they will stick to you, being in no great danger as long as your Majesty hath the force in your hands, being divided into so many hands of your nobility, which is as many lords as there are counties, which is 52, and certainly all those are not likely to agree at one time against you.

Clarendon MS 109, ff. 52–4, Bodleian Library, Oxford.

The Gentry and their Tenants

64　John Houghton, 1682

Prodigality, or Men's spending their estates doth not prejudice the nation

I pray consider the prodigal's life. I will suppose his parents leave him a great estate in land, the income whereof he spends, and borrows more, and when much straitened, mortgages his land for more; then he racks his tenants to pay this interest, which puts him upon new projects and industry how they may live as well then as before; for as our proverb saith, Necessity is the mother of invention. Which projects and industry they never before could be induced to, because their rent was small, and their livelihoods came in, as it did with their forefathers, very easy. Witness the great improvement made of lands since our inhuman civil wars, when our gentry, who before hardly knew what it was to think, then fell to such an industry, and caused such an improvement as England never knew before.

J. Houghton, *A Collection for the Improvement of Husbandry and Trade,* 1728, IV, p. 56.

65　Sir Ralph Verney, 1650

I ever was, and still am, of opinion that no man is bound to suffer his tenants to reap the benefit of his land because they are poor. That were a ready way indeed to make them rich and him poor. Nor is any man tied to let his land (unless it be of great value) [so] as his tenant with his family may live upon the profits of it, for perhaps a man...that takes a farm of £20 rent hath a wife and ten children, and by that time he and they are fed and clothed (though very plainly), I believe there will rest but a small pittance for his landlord. If so, tenants were in a much better condition than their landlords, for they would be sure to have food and raiment when the landlord might be in hazard to want both. But on the other side I do believe a landlord is obliged to take but an equitable rent for his land so as the tenant by God's ordinary providence and blessing upon his honest endeavours may be a gainer by it. And to my knowledge I never broke this rule.

British Museum, Microfilm of Verney MSS, Reel 10.

66   Richard Baxter, 1696

And I humbly motion that gentlemen would not be strangers to their poor tenants; but sometimes go to their houses and see how it goeth with them, and how they live. When I was a child I have heard a poor man praise a neighbour knight with as much honour as if he had been a prince, because he would come to a poor man's house and talk familiarly to them, and look into their pot and cupboard and see how they fared; but a proud, disdainful person none loveth. Did you see their manner of food and labour, and their wants, it would move you more than hearing will do. Strangeness causeth ignorance and neglect.

F.J. Powicke, 'The Reverend Richard Baxter's Last Treatise', *Bulletin John Rylands Library*, x, no. 1, 1926, p. 41.

67   G.M. Trevelyan, 1944

Socially the Restoration restored the nobles and the gentry to their hereditary place as the acknowledged leaders of local and national life. The Englishman's proverbial 'love of a lord', his respectful and admiring interest in 'the squire and his relations', again had full play. Indeed, as events were to prove, the social importance of the peer and the squire, of the gentleman and his lady, was much more completely 'restored' than the power of the King. The Englishman was, at bottom, something of a snob but very little of a courtier....

Nothing marked more clearly the growing power of squirearchy in the House of Commons and in the State than the Game Laws of the Restoration period. By the Forest Laws of Norman and Plantagenet times, the interests of all classes of subjects had been sacrificed in order that the King should have abundance of red deer to hunt; but now the interests of the yeomen and farmers were sacrificed in order that the squire should have plenty of partridges to shoot. Even more than politics, partridges caused neighbours to look at one another askance: for the yeoman free-holder killed, upon his own little farm, the game that wandered over it from the surrounding estates of game preservers. And so in 1671 the Cavalier Parliament passed a law which prevented all freeholders of under a hundred pounds a year—that is to say the very great majority of the class—from killing game, even on their own land. Thus many poor families were robbed of many good meals that were theirs by right; and even those few yeomen whose wealth raised them above the reach of this remarkable law, were for that reason regarded with suspicion. The best that even the good-hearted Sir Roger de Coverley can bring himself to say of the 'yeoman of about a hundred pounds a year', 'who is just within the Game Act', is that 'he would make a good neighbour if he did not destroy so many partridges'—that is to say upon his own land.

For many generations to come, grave social consequences were to flow from the excessive eagerness of the country gentlemen about the preservation of game. Their anxieties on that score had grown with the adoption of the shot-gun. During the Stuart epoch shooting gradually superseded hawking, with the result that birds were more rapidly destroyed, and the supply no longer seemed inexhaustible. In Charles II's reign it was already not unusual to 'shoot flying'. But it was regarded as a difficult art, the more so as it was sometimes practised from horseback. But the 'perching' of pheasants by stalking and shooting them as they sat on the boughs, was still customary among gentlemen.

The netting of birds on the ground was a fashionable sport, often carried on over dogs who pointed the game concealed in the grass. It is written that Sir Roger 'in his youthful days had *taken* forty coveys of partridges in a season' probably by this means. To lure wild duck, by the score and the hundred, into a decoy upon the water's edge was a trade in the fens and a sport on the decoy-pond of the manor house. Liming by twigs, snaring and trapping birds of all kinds, not only pheasants and wild duck but thrushes and fieldfares, had still a prominent place in manuals of *The Gentleman's Recreation.* But the shot-gun was clearly in the ascendant, and with it the tendency to confine sport more and more to the pursuit of certain birds specifically listed as *game.* In that sacred category a place had recently been granted by Statute to grouse and blackcock; already the heather and bracken where they lurked were protected from being burnt except at certain times of the year, and the shepherd transgressing the law was liable to be whipped. Addison's Tory squire declared the new Game Law to be the only good law passed since the Revolution.

English Social History. A survey of six centuries: Chaucer to Queen Victoria, Longmans, 1944, pp. 252, 279–80.

Urban Craftsmen and Town Oligarchies

68   George Unwin, 1904

In tracing backwards the spiritual ancestry of the organized skilled workman of the present day, the first link is undoubtedly to be found in the small master of the seventeenth century. It is in his efforts after organization, partly in their success, but quite as much in their failure, that the immediate antecedents of the modern trade union are to be sought. We have so far been following the history of these efforts along two main lines, the attempt to preserve an active share in the control of the older companies by means of the yeomanry organization or otherwise, and the attempt to secure economic independence through separate incorporation. The movement reached high-water mark in the second of these aspects under the personal government of Charles I, and in the first of them, under the Commonwealth. After that it began perceptibly to ebb. The small master was gradually ousted from his share in the older companies, and the political circumstances were no longer favourable to the formation of new ones. The secret of this retrogressive movement was that transformation of the small master into the journeyman which has already been described. And just as we found the small master in the sixteenth century struggling to adapt and appropriate the traditions of the superseded handicraft organization, so we shall find the journeyman at the close of the seventeenth century endeavouring to build up a new status out of the ruins of the small master. With the clear emergence of this new class, conscious of its special interests and combining effectually for their promotion, our story ends.... But in order to realize the conditions which shaped the later movement we must trace the decay of the constitutional position of the small master....

All facts...adduced in previous chapters tend to show that the industrial protection movement of the Stuart period, though it professed to champion the cause of the small master whose class constituted the industrial democracy of that time, and though it often enlisted his support and was carried to a successful issue with his assistance, was not animated mainly by a regard to his interests, and did not as a matter of fact tend to subserve them. But the victories thus won with his help and in his name, whilst they served in many cases to undermine his economic status, quickened his sense of his rights and kept his capacity for organization alert and vigorous. At the time when the Civil War broke out, the cause of the organized small master as such was to a great extent already a lost cause, and he was within measurable distance of being driven to take his stand with the journeyman class, and to furnish, by virtue of his traditions and of his capacity for social action, the nucleus of a new form of organization.

It is this prophetic significance which lends a peculiar interest to the last heroic stand made by the small master, under the inspiration of that ardent outburst of democratic feeling which signalized the opening of the Commonwealth period. Now for the first time his position in the industrial organization, of which he was nominally a member, might be discussed, not as a matter of vested interest, but as a question of high abstract principle....

It was the day of the 'Levellers' and of the 'Diggers', and there can be no doubt that in the camp of the malcontents there were to be found, not only a mass of small masters fast sinking into the position of workmen, but also a number of that growing class of journeymen which within another twenty years was to be forming organizations of its own. The demand for universal suffrage included the journeymen, who in some companies at least were reckoned as freemen....

The democratic movement within the companies was the rally of a dying cause. As far as its immediate object was concerned, the practical results were very slight. After the Restoration they entirely disappeared, and the older influences resumed complete possession of the disputed ground....

The case which best serves to illustrate the turning-point which has now been reached in the history of industrial organization, is the attempt of the sawyers to gain incorporation in 1670. The sawyers were employed by members of the Carpenters', Joiners', and Shipwrights' Companies; and in 1655 the carpenters had obtained an order from the Lord Mayor's Court for the regulation of their wages. The movement of 1670 is a pretty sure sign of a previously existing combination, and their employers declared that they had raised their price per load during the past twenty-five years from 5s to 6s and then from 6s to 8s and 9s. The nature of the objections successfully raised by the carpenters and others against the sawyers' application, shows clearly how similar the objects of their proposed incorporation were to those of the eighteenth-century trade union. The carpenters in conjunction with the joiners and shipwrights state that the sawyers are labourers who work by the day for wages, or by the load, and that the material is in every case provided by the employer. If they are incorporated, the smallest combination amongst them will bring the building trades to a standstill, as experience has sufficiently shown in the past even without incorporation. Moreover their main object is to exclude 'all those sort of Labourers who daily resort to the city of London and parts adjacent, and by that means keepe the wages and prizes of these sorts of labourers att an equal and indifferent rate' and their success would be 'an evill president, all other Labourers, to Masons, Bricklayers, Plaisterers, &c. having the same reason to alledge for incorporation.'

Here we have a combination of workers endeavouring to appropriate the small masters' method of incorporation to the protection of their own status as wage-earners. Almost at the same moment, a body of wage-earners in another trade is found attempting to use its inherited share in an existing corporation for the same ends. By its failure along these traditional lines, the wage-earning class was driven into secret combinations, from the obscurity of which the trade union did not emerge till the nineteenth century. At this point then, it may be said that the latest phase of the transformed gild and the earliest phase of the trade union meet and blend. . . .

It was the growth of trading capital which, by separating the craftsman from direct contact with the market, gave rise to those intermediate forms of industrial organization which have been grouped together under the term 'domestic system'. The decay of those forms and their ultimate displacement by the factory system was due to the growth of industrial capital. As long as the small master owned most of the industrial capital required for the exercise of his calling, he was not a mere wage-earner, however much he might be dependent on the capital of the trader. With the appearance of the industrial capitalist, who organized manufacture on a large scale and supplied not only the circulating but sometimes also the fixed capital, the small master was reduced either to the position of a journeyman, or to that of a wage-earning master scarcely distinguishable from a journeyman. The strong objection of the London feltmakers to the giving out of materials caused their development to take the first of these forms. But in many widespread industries, including country felt-making, the second form was more common. The Bethnal Green silk-weaver is a wage-earner of this type who still retains some features of the small master, and a large part of the felt-making in the North of England about the middle of the last century was carried on by wage-earning domestic masters who, though they found their own workshops and implements and took apprentices, had come to be called journeymen.

The labour troubles of the eighteenth century, which marked the beginnings of Trade Unionism, were mostly due to the efforts of this class of reduced small masters to organize themselves along with the journeymen on a common footing as wage-earners....

...It has perhaps hardly been sufficiently realized how much the growth of trade unionism in England is due to the prevalence of the principle of *laissez-faire*. It has indeed been rightly insisted upon that there was a close connexion between the abandonment by the Government of the obsolete regulative machinery of the sixteenth century and the rise of combinations amongst the wage-earning class; and no doubt the continuance of similar governmental regulations in France and Germany for some generations longer had much to do with the postponement of trade unionism on the continent. But there is another important aspect of the matter which should not be neglected. The passing of the Combination Acts, and the early prosecutions of trade unionists, should not blind us to the fact that it was the comparative freedom of England in the eighteenth century which alone made the combination of wage-earners possible. At the very moment when the workers of England were laying the foundations of a free organization, by the establishment of the 'tramping ticket' and the 'house of call', the Governments of France and of Prussia were putting a veto on any such spontaneous popular development, by transferring these same institutions into the hands of the police, and utilizing them as part of the machinery of a more or less benevolent despotism.

Industrial Organization in the Sixteenth and Seventeenth Centuries (1904), Cass, 1957, pp. 200–1, 204–5, 210, 212–13, 225–7.

69 Peter Clark and Paul Slack, 1972

The concentration of political power [in towns] itself reflected an overall polarization within urban society affecting not only economic but demographic and social structures. All these factors arise from urban tensions. But the most important cause was exogenous: the Crown was obsessed in the years before 1640 with the need for small knots of reliable men in every town and promoted this policy by the grant or revision of charters, and through widespread conciliar intervention....

Not only was there political conflict within towns at this time but also disputes with outside agencies. One of the most aggressive intruders was the central government. The Crown through charters and legislation enlarged the scope of corporation power within the community so that town governments came to monopolize responsibility for moral and social disciplines, previously shared with ecclesiastical and gild authorities. But if town government was thereby consolidated, the Crown was further concerned with asserting its own control, indirectly through the creation of subservient oligarchies and directly by blows at particular privileges. This last attack reached its climax in the Elizabethan war at the end of the sixteenth century; under the guise of improved efficiency town liberties were overridden by county administrators. When towns drew back from the increasing financial and administrative impositions the Crown retaliated by threatening to annul their charters. Lincoln was warned by the Privy Council in 1596: 'You are to consider that in a time of such necessity as this, it is unfit to stand curiously and precisely upon advantages of privileges, when it is much more fit for every man to put his helping hand to supply the common want'—a concept the medieval townsman would have found it difficult to understand. The exigencies of the end of Elizabeth's reign recurred in the 1620s and in the 1640s with the same damaging disruption of town administration. During the Civil War both parties demonstrated a systematic indifference to the pretensions of corporate privileges.... Overall, there was a blurring of county and town jurisdictions. But we should not exaggerate the effect of the Revolution: it was the period after 1660 that was to see the most vicious onslaught on urban political life.

The purge of magistracy which followed the Corporation Act of 1661 was more wide-sweeping than anything experienced before. While only 4 out of 30 magistrates were excluded in New Windsor, at Gloucester 30 lost their places out of 47, at Shrewsbury 49 out of 73, at Oxford 31 out of 114, and at Leicester 40 out of 72. It is true that sometimes those excluded formally continued to serve, as at Leicester; it is also true that at Chester this purge did not silence the city's vociferous opposition to outside intervention. But in the long run systematic deprivation could only be harmful at a time when in any case fewer men were forthcoming to take up the responsibilities of public office. Moreover, the Restoration upheavals were only a prelude to the *Quo Warranto* attacks which culminated in those of James II's reign; these precipitated political and administrative disorganization in municipal corporations.

Another invasion was mounted by the local gentry. The last years of the seventeenth century saw their final penetration of town politics as parliamentary conflict between county Whig and county Tory was fought out in urban elections. But this was only the last phase of an old and influential experience. Already in the fifteenth century towns had elected gentlemen as burgesses, and after the Reformation with the purchase by gentry families of religious property, another arena for influence and dispute was opened. In the sixteenth-century scramble for land, town estates were attractive plunder to the prospecting gentleman; urban property in the countryside was especially vulnerable to predatory despoilment but even common lands encircling the town were not inviolate. As the central government extended its influence in town politics, its agents (often country gentry) were the ultimate beneficiaries. C.G. Parsloe observes that if the flood of Crown charters freed townsmen from formal subordination to county authorities 'they could not afford protection from the private pressure of county magnates and privy councillors'. As the economic and political balance tipped against a town the favour of a Court or County aristocrat became indispensable for survival: a patron procured a new charter or fair and warded off the most extortionate demands of Whitehall. Only a few towns like prosperous Exeter and Liverpool were able to dispense with their patrons in these years, although most saw the fatal logic. A Leicester man summed up the value of Lord Stamford as patron in 1632: 'He never had done good nor ever would do for he had undone two or three towns.'

The phenomenon of gentlemen burgesses was, as we have said, neither new in 1500 nor absolute by 1700. The picture is uneven. Some towns held out strongly against electing any foreigner, a few succeeded, and others capitulated without more than a token struggle. None the less, these two centuries saw a general takeover of borough seats by country gentlemen....

To conclude, the continuous growth of oligarchic magistracy is the most obvious theme in English urban history from 1500 to 1700. Despite the strength of anti-oligarchic agitation in the decades before 1640 and the incidence of purges during the Revolution there is no evidence that the Civil War and Interregnum led to any broadening of town government. Certainly Cromwellian corporations were as oligarchic as their Royalist forerunners. This persistence of the order of government by clique is an indicator less of internal stability and quietism than of civic friability: few members of the respectable classes dared, in the last analysis, tolerate any major disruption.

Crisis and Order in English Towns, 1500–1700, Routledge, 1972, pp. 22–5.

Education and Social Class

70　The Duke of Newcastle, 1660

After the Reformation and Dissolution of the abbeys, then the
law crept up, and at last grew to be so numerous and to such a
vast body as it swelled to be too big for the kingdom, and hath
been no small means to foment and continue this late and unfortunate rebellion. How to diminish them would be a hard work;
they have taken so deep root in England. To lessen their fees will
not do it. Fewer grammar schools would do well, for if you cut
off much reading and writing, there must be fewer lawyers and so
consequently clerks, which I have been credibly informed that
there are 60,000 clerks at least. What number of lawyers, then?
The nurseries of them should be looked unto, not to be too
many....

The Bible in English under every weaver's and chambermaid's
arms hath done us much hurt. That which made it one way is the
universities. Abounds with too many scholars. Therefore, if every
college had but half the number, they would be better fed and as
well taught. But that which hath done most hurt is the abundance
of grammar schools and inns of courts. The Treasurer Burghley
said there was too many grammar schools, because it made the
plough and the cart be neglected, which was to feed us and defend
us, for there are few that can read that will put their hands to the
plough or the cart, and armies are made of the common soldiers,
and there are very few that can read that will carry a musket. And
there are so many schools now as most read. So indeed there
should be, but such a proportion as to serve the church and
moderately the law and the merchants, and the rest for the labour,
for else they run out to idle and unnecessary people that becomes

a factious burthen to the Commonwealth. For when most was unlettered, it was much a better world both for peace and war.

Clarendon MS 109, ff. 25, 19–20, Bodleian Library, Oxford.

71   Lawrence Stone, 1964

If it is accepted that over half the male population of London was literate, that a high proportion of the one third of adult males who could sign their names in the home counties could read, and that $2\frac{1}{2}$ per cent of the annual male seventeen-year-old age-group was going on to higher education, then the English in 1640 were infinitely better educated than they had been before. It was a quantitative change of such magnitude that it can only be described as a revolution. How the new pattern compared with that of other European countries we simply do not know, for the social history of education has hardly begun. But it may well be that early seventeenth-century England was at all levels the most literate society the world had ever known.

This is speculation, but it is certain that English education did not again reach the same quantitative level for a very, very long time. Belief in linear progress dies hard, but it is no more inevitable in education than in the fields of economics or morals. The decline in numbers at the Universities and the Inns of Court in the late seventeenth century involved a very sharp fall in the proportion of the annual male age-group educated up to this level. When the population started rising after 1740 the proportion began falling even faster, and it was not till after the first World War that it again reached the level of the 1630s. The Robbins Committee estimates that the proportion of the 18-year-old age-group of both sexes entering fulltime University or further education (excluding teacher-training) was 1.2 per cent in 1900 and 2.0 per cent in 1938. Other calculations have been made so as to be more directly comparable with the figures for males only for the 1630s. Taking the census returns of 1931, one fifth of the five-year male age-group fifteen to nineteen gives an eighteen-year-old cohort of 342,000 in England and Wales. 8,720 male students entered Universities in that year, of which it is estimated that only 7,927 were United

Kingdom residents. In 1931 male university entrants formed 2.3 per cent of the age-group, which is about the same percentage as that achieved 300 years earlier. In quantitative terms, English higher education did not get back to the level of the 1630s until after the first World War; did not surpass it until after the second.

Concurrently with the decay in higher education, the tailing off of new endowments of Latin grammar schools after 1660 put an end to their growth, while the multitude of little village schools run by the private enterprise of the parson, curate or free-lance schoolmaster slowly died away. The three Cambridge College admission registers provide ample proof that the eighteenth-century parson had other, if not better, things to do than to educate the local children up to university level. . . .

The causes of the prolonged educational depression which began in the second half of the seventeenth century and lasted for over one hundred years are still largely unknown, and little more can be done than to advance some very tentative suggestions.

The new foundations had been predominantly the result of Protestant, and indeed Puritan, piety, so that the cooling off of religious enthusiasm inevitably reduced the flow of charitable bequests. The triumph of the landed classes over the Crown in the middle and late seventeenth century took the edge off the appetite for office and court service as power shifted back to the shires. For at least half a century, and possibly more, Castiglione's ideal of the cultivated metropolitan lost much of its attraction. The alarming surplus of clergymen over livings, and the deplorably low level of income of many of these livings anyway, must have deterred many parents from directing their children into holy orders. Finally the very marked tightening of the land market in the late seventeenth and eighteenth centuries must have reduced the numbers of *nouveaux riches* seeking to consolidate their new status as landowners by giving their sons a conventional upper-class education. Hence the fall in undergraduate and graduate numbers, which was hardly counterbalanced by the rise of education at the Dissenting Academies or elsewhere.

One might have supposed that the exclusion of dissenters from the Universities after 1660 would have reduced the proportion of entrants from the bourgeoisie. One might also have supposed that this class would have become disillusioned about the value of a gentlemanly, classical training as they gained in self-confidence under the teachings of men like Baxter and Defoe. Though further research is needed on this point, the evidence of St John's and Caius suggests that in fact the reduction in numbers affected the gentry and the rural poor more than the bourgeoisie and urban lower middle class. In view of the progressive inflation of the status of gentleman between the 1630s and 1690s, the decline in numbers of gentry is very striking indeed, particularly at Caius. It looks as if it was the lesser gentry, financially hard-pressed by rising taxation and lagging rents, reluctant to rub shoulders in a College hall with their social inferiors, and alienated from the Court, who were leading the flight from higher education. As Anthony Wood put it: 'After the restauration Oxford did in some manner decay in number: Presbyterians and Independents and other fanaticall people did forbeare to send their sons for feare of orthodox principles. Another party thought an University too low a breeding.'

Education was now regarded with considerable suspicion, being charged with guilt by association with the political and religious upheavals of the previous twenty years. It was thought that too much education of the middle and lower classes had been at the bottom of the trouble, and proof of the theory was found in the schemes for expansion and reform put forward by the Puritans during the Interregnum. In 1678 Christopher Wase had to admit that 'There is an opinion commonly receiv'd that the Scholars of England are overproportion'd to the preferments for letter'd Persons.... But the multiplying these Foundations is yet higher represented as dangerous to the Government. These jealousies have gain'd upon the Prudent, the Powerful, and not least upon the Scholar.' It was widely believed that classical education should in future be confined to gentlemen by restricting the number of free places for the poor at grammar schools and Universities. 'The Gentry require that such as would have the Liberall Arts and Sciences should pay for them: without censure [to] keep their blood unmixt with mean conversation.' In this post-Restoration period can be seen the crystallization of that all too familiar English association of educational opportunity with social status. This restrictive view was merely part of the wider swing back to extreme conservatism which both characterized and made possible the Restoration. In the church and the Universities, Laudianism and scholasticism triumphed once more. Electoral reform, law reform, educational reform, educational expansion and puritanism all went down together, only to re-emerge as powerful forces in English life some two hundred years later.

'The educational revolution in England, 1540–1640', *Past and Present*, no. 28, 1964, pp. 68–9, 73–5.

72   Lawrence Stone, 1969

One of the most significant indications of the 'open' or 'closed' character of a society is whether the movement from one educational level to another is a regulated trickle, as in early modern England with its modest provision for grammar school and university scholarships; or a competitive trickle, as in eighteenth- and nineteenth-century France with its concourse to the *Grandes Ecoles*; or a competitive flood, as in twentieth-century America. . . .

   In England after the Restoration, many of the propertied classes followed Hobbes in blaming the horrors of the Civil War on excessive education in the pre-war years. Between 1660 and 1790 most men were convinced that a little learning for the poor is a dangerous thing, since it encourages them to aspire beyond their station, and so threatens social stability and the domination of the élite. In the late seventeenth century Francis Osborne concluded magisterially that 'A too universally dilated learning hath bin found upon Trial in all Ages no fast friend to Policy or Religion; being no less ready to discover blemishes in the one then Incongruities in the other'—an opinion summed up by his opponent Christopher Wase as the principle that 'Ignorance is the Mother of Devotion and Obedience'. This was a view which it took a very long time to eradicate, and may be traced through Bernard Mandeville's comment in the early eighteenth century that 'should a Horse know as much as a Man, I should not like to be his Rider' and Soame Jenyns's complacent view of popular ignorance in 1757 as the opiate of the poor, 'a cordial administered by the gracious hand of providence', right down to the opinion of Bishop Beilby Porteous of London in 1803 that 'men of considerable ability say that it is safest for both the Government and the religion of the country to let the lower classes remain in that state of ignorance in which nature has originally placed them'. . . .

Between 1680 and 1780 there was a marked slowing down of growth in basic literacy due to fear among the upper classes that popular education was a contributory factor in causing the revolutionary activity of the 1640s and '50s; and a significant decline in classical secondary and university education due to a reaction against formalistic training in Latin by the middle classes, to a closing up of the avenues of advancement through these channels, and to a withdrawal of the upper classes to education at home and on the Grand Tour to avoid moral and social contamination in educational institutions. On the other hand, instruction of the lower middle classes in both the three Rs and in technical education for account-keeping, surveying etc. continued to grow fairly rapidly. . . .

The slowing up of the growth of literacy in England after 1670 allowed the parson and the squire to re-establish their predominant role in the village as the source of ideological, religious and social ideas, and so helped to ensure domestic peace for about a century.

'Literacy and education in England, 1640–1900', *Past and Present*, no. 42, 1969, pp. 73–4, 85, 136–8.

Theories of Social Class

73   R.B. Schlatter, 1940

Religious writers welcomed the hereditary ranks, privileges, and fortunes, which they thought were necessary for subjection and obedience. If all men were equal, there could be no government in the world. Some persons must be given the power, the dignity, and the respect necessary to direct and rule their neighbours. Equality would breed confusion, since no man would consent to obey his equal.

Secondly, inequality was said to be necessary for trade, industry, and the arts. The majority of men would not work unless they were compelled, and no one would undertake the hardest labours. Division of effort would be impossible, and inefficiency would be the result of the lack of prudent administration.

In order to reinforce the psychological impulses which caused individuals to choose various vocations naturally, Divine Providence set up the social hierarchy. By this arrangement, interest prompted the upper classes to rule and direct the poor, while the latter found it beneficial to themselves to obey the rich. The king himself could not live if the poor did not work for him, while they could not live without the help of the rich. While gentlemen are relieved from drudgery, the labourers are given employment and direction. Thus all classes are mutually helpful. In the words of Isaac Barrow:

> So hath the great author of order distributed the ranks and offices of men in order to mutual benefit and comfort, that one man should plow, another thresh... another sail, another trade, another supervise all these, labouring to keep them all in order

and peace; that one should work with his hands and feet, another with his head and tongue, all conspiring to one common end, the welfare of the whole.

Finally, in a society in which ranks are based on an unequal distribution of property, Christian virtues could most readily be exercised. The rich are given the opportunity of being charitable, the poor can be patient, and men of moderate fortune are able to be content. Without inequality of wealth, and a recognition that the various classes have varying duties to perform, the most important virtues of religion would be disused.

The whole case for ranks and unequal division of wealth was well put by George Hickes, Dean of Worcester, in a sermon before the Mayor and Aldermen of London on 1 April 1684.

'Civil Equality', he said, 'is morally impossible, because no commonweal, little or great, can subsist without poor. They are necessary for the establishment of superiority and subjection in humane societies, where there must be members of dishonor as well as honor, and some to serve and obey, as well as others to command. The poor are the hands and feet of the body politick . . . who hew the wood, and draw the water of the rich. They plow our lands, and dig our quarries, and cleanse our streets, nay, those who fight our battels in the defence of their country are the poor souldiers. . . . But were all equally rich, there would be no subordination, none to command, nor none to serve.'

Hickes went on to recommend the virtue of charity, for the rich, and humility, for the poor.

Thus, by a happy arrangement of Divine Providence, human society was knit together by a bond of mutual benefit. If all ranks of men performed their duties, every individual would profit. But this desirable result depended upon classes, with their various duties and privileges, being clearly defined, and being accepted and respected by all. . . .

So the classical hierarchical theory continued to be current in the reign of Charles II. But whereas the theory assumed that class structure was static, in fact, English society had for two centuries been increasingly fluid. New classes were rising, old ones were being transformed. In the course of our discussion of these various classes we must bear in mind this relatively new factor of fluidity.

The Social Ideas of Religious Leaders, 1660–1688, Oxford University Press, 1940, pp. 107–10.

Part Six

MANNERS, MORALS, AND THE MIRROR OF LITERATURE

Contemporaries were agreed that changes in manners and social attitudes occurred during the Interregnum, which ultimately wrought a deeper transformation in codes of behaviour and standards of morality. Clarendon (74) enumerated various influences at work: the less formal social behaviour of the sectaries who deprecated deference and conceded an unaccustomed freedom of action to women; the insidious and corrupting influence of conspiracy and deceit which was rife during the war and continued in the following years of political uncertainty; the elation which followed the Restoration, and encouraged men to indulge in pleasure; and the mood of the king, disillusioned by his place-seeking, quarrelsome supporters.

Merrymaking was not all loss, however; it had its political uses. While it was a conscious and deliberate reaction against Puritanism, it was also recognized as a useful outlet for energies that might otherwise have been channelled into fresh factions and rebellions. The Duke of Newcastle expressed this view candidly (75).

Macaulay (76) maintained that licentious indulgence was almost inevitable when the Puritan reins were loosened. He found its rationale in the theories of Thomas Hobbes for Hobbes took from the individual responsibility for his beliefs and his behaviour and left everything to be determined by the sovereign. At the same time he blamed the Church for failing to take a firm stand on moral issues; it was waging war too energetically on schism to have time to make war on vice. In a review of some Restoration plays, Macaulay (77) delivered an even more forceful tirade against the decline of morals, seizing the chance to drive home the lesson that politicians can never successfully *enforce* godliness.

Trevelyan (78) accepted the views of Clarendon on moral standards, but carefully restricted the latter's generalizations to the upper classes. He blamed the Restoration dramatists for the survival into the present century of Puritanical attitudes to the theatre. But does not the survival of Puritanism itself explain it better?

Restoration literature reflected current upper-class morality, but it also reflected the unusually strong personal influence of Charles II. In his years abroad, Charles imbibed European cultural tastes. He had a more European Catholic outlook on life and leisure than any earlier English monarch, and his preferences matched the mood of the new age. But he offered more than mere approving patronage. James Sutherland (79) describes Charles's direct responsibility for some of the literary styles and productions of the Restoration. He also sums up the literary achievements of the Restoration, taking a broader viewpoint (80), embracing not only poets and playwrights, but essayists, diarists, scholars, and political and religious writers.

Manners and Morals

74   Lord Clarendon, 1672

All relations were confounded by the several sects in religion, which discountenanced all forms of reverence and respect, as reliques and marks of superstition. Children asked not blessing of their parents; nor did they concern themselves in the education of their children, but were well content that they should take any course to maintain themselves, that they might be free from that expense. The young women conversed without any circumspection or modesty, and frequently met at taverns and common eating-houses, and they who were stricter and more severe in their comportment, became the wives of the seditious preachers or of officers of the army. The daughters of noble and illustrious families bestowed themselves upon the divines of the time, or other low and unequal matches. Parents had no manner of authority over their children, nor children any obedience or submission to their parents; but every one did that which was good in his own eyes. This unnatural antipathy had its first rise from the beginning of the rebellion, when the fathers and sons engaged themselves in the contrary parties, the one choosing to serve the King, and the other the Parliament; which division and contradiction of affections was afterwards improved to mutual animosities and direct malice, by the help of the preachers and the several factions in religion, or by the absence of all religion; so that there were never such examples of impiety between such relations in any age of the world, Christian or heathen, as that wicked time from the beginning of the Rebellion to the King's return; of which the families of Hotham and Vane are sufficient instances, though other more illustrious houses may be named, where the same accursed fruit was too plentifully gathered, and too notorious to the world. The relation between masters and servants had been long since dissolved by the Parliament, that their army might be increased by the prentices against their masters' consent, and that they might have intelligence of the secret meetings and transactions in those houses and families which were not devoted to them; from whence issued the foulest treacheries and perfidiousness that were ever practised. And the blood of the master was frequently the price of the servant's villany....

In a word, the nation was corrupted from that integrity, good nature and generosity that had been peculiar to it, and for which it had been signal and celebrated throughout the world; in the room whereof the vilest craft and dissembling had succeeded. The tenderness of the bowels which is the quintessence of justice and compassion, the very mention of good nature, was laughed at and looked upon as the mark and character of a fool; and a roughness of manners, or hardheartedness and cruelty was affected. In the place of generosity, a vile and sordid love of money was entertained as the truest wisdom, and anything lawful that would contribute towards being rich. There was a total decay, or rather a final expiration, of all friendship and to dissuade a man from any thing he affected, or to reprove him for anything he had done amiss, or to advise him to do anything he had no mind to do, was thought an impertinence unworthy a wise man, and received with reproach and contempt. These dilapidations and ruins of the ancient candour and discipline were not taken enough to heart, and repaired with that early care and severity that they might have been; for they were not then incorrigible....

'He [Charles II] could not but observe* that the whole nation seemed to him a little corrupted in their excess of living. All men spend much more in their clothes, in their diet, in all their expenses, than they had used to do. He hoped it had only been the excess of joy after so long sufferings that had transported him and them to those other excesses, but, he desired them, 'that they might all take heed that the continuance of them did not indeed corrupt their natures. He did believe that he had been that way very faulty himself; he promised that he would reform, and that if they would

*Clarendon here reports Charles II's speech to Parliament at the prorogation, 19 May 1662.

join with him in their several capacities, they would by their examples do more good, both in city and country, than any new laws would do.' He said many other good things that pleased them, and no doubt he intended all he said, but the ways and expedients towards good husbandry were nowhere pursued. . . .

Most men [i.e. in the Royalist party] were affected and more grieved and discontented for any honour and preferment which they saw conferred upon another man than for being disappointed in their own particular expectations; and looked upon every obligation bestowed upon another man, how meritorious soever, as upon a reproach to them, and an upbraiding of their want of merit.

This unhappy temper and constitution of the royal party, with whom he had always intended to have made a firm conjunction against all accidents and occurrences which might happen at home or from abroad, did wonderfully displease and trouble the king, and with the other perplexities which are mentioned before, did so break his mind, and had that operation upon his spirits that, finding he could not propose any such method to himself, by which he might extricate himself out of those many difficulties and labyrinths in which he was involved, nor expedite those important matters which depended upon the good will and dispatch of the Parliament, which would proceed by its own rules, and with its accustomed formalities, he grew more disposed to leave all things to their natural course and God's providence, and, by degrees, unbent his mind from the knotty and ungrateful part of his business, grew more remiss in his application to it, and indulged to his youth and appetite that license and satisfaction that it desired, and for which he had opportunity enough, and could not be without ministers abundant for any such negotiations, the time itself, and the young people thereof of either sex having been educated in all the liberty of vice without reprehension or restraint.

The Life of Edward Earl of Clarendon, written by Himself, 3rd edn, Oxford, 1761, II, pp. 39–41, 315, 38–9.

75   The Duke of Newcastle, 1660

Recreations and festivals

First for London, Paris Garden will hold good for the meaner people. Then for several playhouses, as there were five at least in my time...but five or six playhouses is enough for all sorts of people's diversion and pleasure in that kind. Then puppet plays there will be to please them, besides as also dancers of the ropes, with jugglers and tumblers, besides strange sights of beasts, birds, monsters, and many other things, which several sorts of music and dancing and all the old holidays with their mirth and rites set up again, feasting daily will be in merry England, for England is so plentiful of all provision that if we do not eat them, they will eat us, so we feast in our own defence.

For the Country Recreations

May games, Morris dances, the Lord of the May and Lady of the May, the fool and the Hoby Horse must not be forgotten, also Whitsun Lord and Lady, thrashing of hens at Shrove Tide, carols and wassails at Christmas, with good plum porridge and pies which now are forbidden as profane, ungodly things, wakes, fairs and markets maintains commerce and trade, and after evening prayer every Sunday and Holy Day the country people, with their fresher lasses, to trip on the town green about the maypole to the louder bagpipe there to be refreshed with their ale and cakes...these divertisments will amuse the people's thoughts and keep them in harmless actions which will free your Majesty from faction and rebellion.

Clarendon MS 109, ff. 74–5, Bodleian Library, Oxford.

76 Lord Macaulay, 1848

A change still more important took place in the morals and manners of the community. Those passions and tastes which, under the rule of the Puritans, had been sternly repressed, and, if gratified at all, had been gratified by stealth, broke forth with ungovernable violence as soon as the check was withdrawn. Men flew to frivolous amusements and to criminal pleasures with the greediness which long and enforced abstinence naturally produces. Little restraint was imposed by public opinion. For the nation, nauseated with cant, suspicious of all pretensions to sanctity, and still smarting from the recent tyranny of rulers austere in life and powerful in prayer, looked for a time with complacency on the softer and gayer vices. Still less restraint was imposed by the government. Indeed there was no excess which was not encouraged by the ostentatious profligacy of the King and of his favourite courtiers. A few counsellors of Charles the First, who were now no longer young, retained the decorous gravity which had been thirty years before in fashion at Whitehall. Such were Clarendon himself, and his friends, Thomas Wriothesley, Earl of Southampton, Lord Treasurer, and James Butler, Duke of Ormond, who, having through many vicissitudes struggled gallantly for the royal cause in Ireland, now governed that kingdom as Lord Lieutenant. But neither the memory of the services of these men, nor their great power in the state, could protect them from the sarcasms which modish vice loves to dart at obsolete virtue. The praise of politeness and vivacity could now scarcely be obtained except by some violation of decorum. Talents great and various assisted to spread the contagion. Ethical philosophy had recently taken a form well suited to please a generation equally devoted to monarchy and to vice. Thomas Hobbes had, in language more precise and luminous than has ever been employed by any other metaphysical writer, maintained that the will of the prince was the standard of right and wrong, and that every subject ought to be ready to profess Popery, Mahometanism, or Paganism, at the royal command. Thousands who were incompetent to appreciate what was really valuable in his speculations, eagerly welcomed a theory which, while it exalted the kingly office, relaxed the obligations of morality, and degraded religion into a mere affair of state. Hobbism soon became an almost essential part of the character of the fine gentleman. All the lighter kinds of literature were deeply tainted by the prevailing licentiousness. Poetry stooped to be the pandar of every low desire. Ridicule, instead of putting guilt and error to the blush, turned her formidable shafts against innocence and truth. The restored Church contended indeed against the prevailing immorality, but contended feebly, and with half a heart. It was necessary to the decorum of her character that she should admonish her erring children: but her admonitions were given in a somewhat perfunctory manner. Her attention was elsewhere engaged. Her whole soul was in the work of crushing the Puritans, and of teaching her disciples to give unto Caesar the things which were Caesar's. She had been pillaged and oppressed by the party which preached an austere morality. She had been restored to opulence and honour by libertines. Little as the men of mirth and fashion were disposed to shape their lives according to her precepts, they were yet ready to fight knee deep in blood for her cathedrals and palaces, for every line of her rubric and every thread of her vestments. If the debauched Cavalier haunted brothels and gambling houses, he at least avoided conventicles. If he never spoke without uttering ribaldry and blasphemy, he made some amends by his eagerness to send Baxter and Howe to gaol for preaching and praying. Thus the clergy, for a time, made war on schism with so much vigour that they had little leisure to make war on vice. The ribaldry of Etherege and Wycherley was, in the presence and under the special sanction of the head of the Church, publicly recited by female lips in female ears, while the author of the Pilgrim's Progress languished in a dungeon for the crime of proclaiming the gospel to the poor. It is an unquestionable and a most instructive fact that the years during which the political power of the Anglican hierarchy was in the zenith were precisely the years during which national virtue was at the lowest point.

The History of England from the Accession of James the Second by Lord Macaulay (1848), ed. C.H. Firth, Macmillan, 1913–15, I, pp. 160–2.

Restoration Literature

77   Lord Macaulay, 1841

This part of our literature [Restoration drama] is a disgrace to our language and our national character. It is clever, indeed, and very entertaining; but it is, in the most emphatic sense of the words, 'earthly, sensual, devilish'. Its indecency, though perpetually such as is condemned not less by the rules of good taste than by those of morality, is not, in our opinion, so disgraceful a fault as its singularly inhuman spirit. We have here Belial, not as when he inspired Ovid and Ariosto, 'graceful and humane', but with the iron eye and cruel sneer of Mephistopheles. We find ourselves in a world, in which the ladies are like very profligate, impudent and unfeeling men, and in which the men are too bad for any place but Pandaemonium or Norfolk Island. We are surrounded by foreheads of bronze, hearts like the nether millstone, and tongues set on fire of hell.

. . . The crime charged is not mere coarseness of expression. The terms which are delicate in one age become gross in the next. The diction of the English version of the Pentateuch is sometimes such as Addison would not have ventured to imitate; and Addison, the standard of moral purity in his own age, used many phrases which are now proscribed. Whether a thing shall be designated by a plain noun-substantive or by a circumlocution is mere matter of fashion. Morality is not at all interested in the question. But morality is deeply interested in this, that what is immoral shall not be presented to the imagination of the young and susceptible in constant connection with what is attractive. For every person who has observed the operation of the law of association in his own mind and in the minds of others knows that whatever is constantly presented to the imagination in connection with what is attractive will itself become attractive. There is undoubtedly a great deal of indelicate writing in Fletcher and Massinger, and more than might be wished even in Ben Jonson and Shakespeare, who are comparatively pure. But it is impossible to trace in their plays any systematic attempt to associate vice with those things which men value most and desire most, and virtue with every thing ridiculous and degrading. And such a systematic attempt we find in the whole dramatic literature of the generation which followed the return of Charles the Second. We will take, as an instance of what we mean, a single subject of the highest importance to the happiness of mankind, conjugal fidelity. We can at present hardly call to mind a single English play, written before the civil war, in which the character of a seducer of married women is represented in a favourable light. We remember many plays in which such persons are baffled, exposed, covered with derision, and insulted by triumphant husbands. . . . In general we will venture to say that the dramatists of the age of Elizabeth and James the First either treat the breach of the marriage-vow as a serious crime, or, if they treat it as matter for laughter, turn the laugh against the gallant.

On the contrary, during the forty years which followed the Restoration, the whole body of the dramatists invariably represent adultery, we do not say as a peccadillo, we do not say as an error which the violence of passion may excuse, but as the calling of a fine gentleman, as a grace without which his character would be imperfect. It is as essential to his breeding and to his place in society that he should make love to the wives of his neighbours as that he should know French, or that he should have a sword at his side. In all this there is no passion, and scarcely anything that can be called preference. The hero intrigues just as he wears a wig; because, if he did not, he would be a queer fellow, a city prig, perhaps a Puritan. All the agreeable qualities are always given to the gallant. All the contempt and aversion are the portion of the unfortunate husband. . . .

It must, indeed, be acknowledged, in justice to the writers of whom we have spoken thus severely, that they were to a great extent the creatures of their age. And if it be asked why that age encouraged immorality which no other age would have tolerated, we have no hesitation in answering that this great depravation of the national taste was the effect of the prevalence of Puritanism under the Commonwealth.

To punish public outrages on morals and religion is unquestionably within the competence of rulers. But when a government, not content with requiring decency, requires sanctity, it oversteps the bounds which mark its proper functions. And it may be laid down as a universal rule that a government which attempts more than it ought will perform less. A lawgiver who, in order to protect distressed borrowers, limits the rate of interest, either makes it impossible for the objects of his care to borrow at all, or places them at the mercy of the worst class of usurers. A lawgiver who, from tenderness for labouring men, fixes the hours of their work and the amount of their wages, is certain to make them far more wretched than he found them. And so a government which, not content with repressing scandalous excesses, demands from its subjects fervent and austere piety, will soon discover that, while attempting to render an impossible service to the cause of virtue, it has in truth only promoted vice.

For what are the means by which a government can effect its ends? Two only, reward and punishment; powerful means, indeed, for influencing the exterior act, but altogether impotent for the purpose of touching the heart. A public functionary who is told that he will be promoted if he is a devout Catholic, and turned out of his place if he is not, will probably go to mass every morning, exclude meat from his table on Fridays, shrive himself regularly, and perhaps let his superiors know that he wears a hair shirt next his skin. Under a Puritan government, a person who is apprised that piety is essential to thriving in the world will be strict in the observance of the Sunday, or, as he will call it, Sabbath, and will avoid a theatre as if it were plague-stricken. Such a show of religion as this the hope of gain and the fear of loss will produce, at a week's notice, in any abundance which a government may require. But under this show, sensuality, ambition, avarice, and hatred retain unimpaired power, and the seeming convert has only added to the vices of a man of the world all the still darker vices which are engendered by the constant practice of dissimulation. The truth cannot be long concealed. The public discovers that the grave persons who are proposed to it as patterns are more utterly destitute of moral principle and of moral sensibility than avowed libertines. It sees that these Pharisees are farther removed from real goodness than publicans and harlots. And, as usual, it rushes to the extreme opposite to that which it quits. It considers a high religious profession as a sure mark of meanness and depravity. On the very first day on which the restraint of fear is taken away, and on which men can venture to say what they think, a frightful peal of blasphemy and ribaldry proclaims that the short-sighted policy which aimed at making a nation of saints has made a nation of scoffers.

. . . It is quite certain that, even if the royal family had never returned, even if Richard Cromwell or Henry Cromwell had been at the head of the administration, there would have been a great relaxation of manners. Before the Restoration many signs indicated that a period of licence was at hand. The Restoration crushed for a time the Puritan party, and placed supreme power in the hands of a libertine. The political counter-revolution assisted the moral counter-revolution, and was in turn assisted by it. A period of wild and desperate dissoluteness followed. Even in remote manor-houses and hamlets the change was in some degree felt; but in London the outbreak of debauchery was appalling; and in London the places most deeply infected were the Palace, the quarters inhabited by the aristocracy, and the Inns of Court. It was on the support of these parts of the town that the playhouses depended. The character of the drama became conformed to the character of its patrons. The comic poet was the mouthpiece of the most deeply corrupted part of a corrupted society. And in the plays before us we find, distilled and condensed, the essential spirit of the fashionable world during the anti-Puritan reaction. . . .

In the old drama there had been much that was reprehensible. But. . . the profligacy which follows a period of overstrained austerity goes beyond the profligacy which precedes such a period. The nation resembled the demoniac in the New Testament. The Puritans boasted that the unclean spirit was cast out. The house was empty, swept, and garnished; and for a time the expelled tenant wandered through dry places seeking rest and finding none. But the force of the exorcism was spent. The fiend returned to his abode; and returned not alone. He took to him seven other spirits more wicked than himself. They entered in, and dwelt together: and the second possession was worse than the first.

'Dramatists of the Restoration', in *Essays and Belles Lettres,* Everyman edition, II, pp. 414–15, 419–20, 422–3.

78 G.M. Trevelyan, 1944

At that time a hard-hearted and cynical frivolity prevailed in Whitehall and Westminster much more than in England as a whole. The men who haunted Charles II's Court, the first leaders of the Whig and Tory parties in the time of the Popish Plot and the Exclusion Bill, laughed at all forms of virtue as hypocrisy, and believed that every man had his price.

> What makes all doctrines plain and clear?
> *About two hundred pounds a year.*
> And that which was proved true before
> Prove false again? *Two hundred more.*
>
> (*Hudibras*)

So they thought, being themselves for sale. Yet two thousand Puritan Ministers had just given up their livings and gone out to endure persecution for conscience sake (1662), following the example of their enemies the Anglican clergy who had suffered like things for twenty years past rather than desert the Church in her extremity. The Puritan and Anglican clergy who refused to save their livelihoods by recantation were nearly ten times as numerous as the Catholic and Protestant clergy who had similarly stood out during the frequent Tudor changes of religion. Conscience meant more, not less, than of old. England was sound enough. But her courtiers and politicians were rotten. For the King himself and the younger generation of the aristocracy had been demoralized by the break-up of their education and family life, by exile and confiscation leading to the mean shifts of sudden poverty, by the endurance of injustice done to them in the name of religion, by the constant spectacle of oaths and covenants lightly taken and lightly broken, and all the base underside of revolution and counter-revolution of which they had been the victims.

For these reasons a hard disbelief in virtue of any kind was characteristic of the restored leaders of politics and fashion, and was reflected in the early Restoration drama which depended on their patronage. One of the most successful pieces was Wycherley's *Country Wife*; the hero, by pretending to be a eunuch, secures admission to privacies which enable him to seduce women; one is expected to admire his character and proceedings. In no other age, before or after, would such a plot-motive have appealed to any English audience.

However, the theatre had been restored, and much of its work was good. It revived plays by Shakespeare and Ben Jonson. It was adorned by the poetic genius of Dryden's dramas and the musical genius of Purcell's incidental tunes and operatic pieces. And in the following generation Wycherley's brutalities went clean out of fashion. They were succeeded by the new English comedy of Congreve and Farquhar. Those great writers are usually lumped with Wycherley as 'Restoration Dramatists', but in fact it would be more chronologically correct to call Congreve and Farquhar 'Revolution Dramatists', for they wrote in the reigns of William and Anne.

So the Wycherley period of the English stage did not last long, but it had done permanent harm, because it had confirmed many pious and decent-minded families, High Church as well as Low, in a hostile attitude to the drama, which had in Shakespeare's time been peculiar to rigid Puritans. Till late in the Nineteenth Century, not a few well brought up young people were never allowed to visit the theatre. And if such stringency was the exception rather than the rule, it is at least true to say that the serious part of the nation would never take the theatre seriously. This misfortune was not a little due to Puritan bigotry and to its outcome in the licentiousness of the early Restoration drama. These unhappy conditions were peculiar to England: the age of Wycherley over here was the age of Molière, Corneille and Racine in France. There the drama, comic as well as tragic, was decent and was serious, and the French have ever since taken their drama seriously, as the Elizabethan English took theirs, regarding it as a civilizing influence and a criticism of life.

English Social History, 1944, pp. 260–2.

79   James Sutherland, 1963

Yet however little he [Charles II] wrote and however much or little he may have read, this leisurely and witty king had an influence on the literature of his country such as no other English monarch has had, with the exception of Elizabeth I. The writers of the Restoration period were conscious of Charles II less as the father of his people than as an easy-going uncle, who liked to be amused and who was very well able to distinguish good amusement from bad. Many of the best writers of the day, such as Buckingham, Rochester, Dorset, or Sedley were his familiar companions; others, such as Dryden, Pepys, Evelyn, Wycherley, or Burnet met and conversed with him fairly frequently. No king was ever more easy of access. . . .

The impact of Charles II on the literature of his reign is seen most clearly in the drama. As a habitual playgoer he knew what he liked, and he took some trouble to see that he got what he wanted. What he usually wanted was comedy, which gave him 'the greatest pleasure he had from the Stage.' From time to time he suggested to his dramatists where they could find a good plot. He drew the attention of Sir Samuel Tuke to the Spanish play from which he fashioned *The Adventures of Five Hours*, and near the end of his life he gave Crowne the plot for his *Sir Courtly Nice* by advising him to read Moreto's *No Puede Ser*. From one of Dryden's few surviving letters, we learn that he was at work on a comedy that was to be 'almost such another piece of business as the fond Husband [i.e., Durfey's *The Fond Husband*, 1677], for such the King will have it, who is parcell poet with me in the plott; one of the designes being a story he·was pleasd formerly to tell me. . . .' Charles E. Ward is almost certainly right in identifying this comedy as *Mr Limberham, or the Kind Keeper*. No doubt there were other occasions when the king dropped a hint which a Tuke or a Crowne regarded as 'a sacred command.' Such evidence as is available certainly suggests that he had an eye for a good comic plot.

Left to himself, he might have been prepared to settle for comedy or opera; but he had to consider the tastes of the ladies of the court, and there is a good deal of evidence to show that the female part of a Restoration audience had a decided preference for tragedies and heroic plays. So far as the establishment of the rhymed heroic play in England is concerned, the influence of the king appears to have been decisive, and it can be documented in some detail. His chief instrument in this palace revolution was Roger Boyle, Earl of Orrery. According to Orrery's first biographer,

> King Charles was the first who put my lord upon writing plays, which his majesty did upon occasion of a dispute that arose in his royal presence about writing plays in rhyme: some affirmed it was not to be done; others said it would spoil the fancy to be so confined, but the Lord Orrery was of another opinion; and his majesty being willing a trial should be made, com-manded his lordship to employ some of his leisure that way, which my lord readily did.

To this may be added a statement by the earl himself that he had been commanded by the king to write a play for him and had thereupon written a tragi-comedy in rhyming verse, and 'writt it in that manner...Because I found his majesty Relish'd rather the French Fassion of Playes than the English...'. As Orrery's editor makes clear, this play was *The Generall*, and Orrery must be given what credit is due to the author of the first rhymed heroic play in English. On 26 February 1663, the king wrote to him in encourag-ing terms:

> I will now tell you, that I have read your first play, which I like very well, and doe intend to bring it upon the Stage, as Soone as my Company have their new Stage in order, that the Seanes may bee worthy the words they are to sett forth....

For reasons not entirely clear, *The Generall* was not produced at this time; but, as his editor claims, 'the king's liking for Orrery's unique creation instigated the introduction of the heroic couplet and of disputative scenes concerned with love *vs.* honor, as new fashions in dramatic expression.' When, in the autumn of 1665, Orrery proceeded by the king's command to write another heroic play, *The Black Prince*, and sent the king a specimen of what he had already written, he was again encouraged by a letter that could only have come from Charles II....

One would like to think that the king was being no more than polite when he praised Orrery's plays; and certainly their high-flown sentiments, romantically generous motives, and long introspective debates are very far removed from the shrewd and cynical good sense of Charles II. But it may be that the heroic play with its autocratic and even tyrannical monarchs, its grandiose court settings, and its glorification of power and beauty, gratified a side of Charles II that is rarely noticed, but that became more obvious in the later and more Machiavellian years of his reign, when he ruled without a parliament and with the aid of such men as Sunderland and Jeffreys. However easy-going Charles might seem, there was something in his character which led him toward a more absolute form of government than the vast majority of his subjects would have approved; if he had not actually dreams of glory, he looked with approval, and perhaps envy, at the firm and undemocratic rule of the Grand Monarch across the Channel. His love of comedy may reflect the affable, and even democratic, aspects of the king's character; but his apparent interest in the heroic play (whose absurdities and unreality would seem to be so alien to his realistic appraisal of human character and motives) may reflect his desire for a world in which kings are not constantly checked and obstructed by their subjects.*

There remains one other sphere in which, rather surprisingly, the king exerted a considerable influence. As Defender of the Faith, Charles could not escape listening fairly frequently to sermons, and he liked them to be 'clear, plain, and short.' He had a pronounced dislike of sermons that were read from a manuscript in the pulpit, or even those preached from copious notes. Annoyed in October 1674 by a Cambridge don who preached before him in this manner while he was at Newmarket, he instructed the Duke of Monmouth, who was chancellor at the time, to give orders that all university preachers should have their sermon *memoriter*. A similar direction was given to Oxford in the following month. So far as Charles II was concerned, the ecclesiastical actor had to be perfect in his part. At all events, some of the greatest preachers of the day, like Burnet or South, delivered their sermons *ex tempore*

---

* I owe this suggestion to my colleague, Basil Greenslade, who has also drawn my attention to the way in which the chronically impoverished king employed Hugh May the architect to refurbish Windsor Castle, together with the painter Verrio and a whole army of Italian and French craftsmen and the English Grinling Gibbons. Charles II was not indifferent to the pomp that should surround a monarch.

or from memory, and the liveliness of the Restoration pulpit may be due in considerable measure to this practice. That the king's dislike of the written discourse was well known is suggested by the delightful story of a conversation he is said to have had with Stillingfleet. Why, the king asked, did Stillingfleet always read his sermons when he preached before him, although he invariably preached without notes on other occasions? Stillingfleet replied that 'the awe of so noble an audience, where he saw nothing that was not greatly superior to him, but chiefly the seeing before him so great and wise a prince, made him afraid to trust himself.' He then asked the king why, when he could have none of those reasons, he always read his speeches to Parliament. 'I have asked them so often and for so much money,' the king replied, 'that I am ashamed to look them in the face.'

Whether this anecdote is true or false, it offers us a clue to the kind of influence Charles II must have had on the literature of his age. A king about whom such stories could be recorded—or made up—was clearly a source of inspiration to the writers of the day. So long as Charles II was alive, wit, humor, raillery, repartee, the droll remark, the well-turned phrase were all in demand and certain to be appreciated: the king and his court might be un-friendly to epic, but they were kind to epigram, and the stimulus of a king 'who never said a foolish thing' radiated outward to coffee-house and tavern and to the writer in his study. Rightly or wrongly, Dryden gaves Charles much of the credit for reforming the conversation of Englishmen.

> The desire of imitating so great a pattern first awakened the dull and heavy spirits of the English from their natural reserved-ness; loosened them from their stiff forms of conversation, and made them easy and pliant to each other in discourse. Thus, insensibly, our way of living became more free; and the fire of the English wit, which was being stifled under a constrained, melancholy way of breeding, began first to display its force, by mixing the solidity of our nation with the air and gaiety of our neighbours. [*Essays*, 1, 176]

The significance of this improved conversation and heightened wit for the drama, and more particularly for comedy, is sufficiently obvious, and Dryden goes on to make the point himself. The dramatists wrote better because they had the king and his court as models for imitation, as standards by which to test their own performance, and as judges of the finished work. It is equally true that the prestige of wit led to a swarm of amateur writers who, as Dryden put it, were 'ambitious to distinguish themselves from the herd of gentlemen' by attempting a poem or even a play, and who would have done much better to be 'contented with what fortune has done for them, and sit down quietly with their estates.' But that was the penalty that had to be paid in a period of wit and epigram. If there were inevitably many more Witwouds than Mirabells, the Mirabells were sometimes brilliant, and at least the Witwouds kept on trying.

'The impact of Charles II on Restoration literature', in *Restoration and Eighteenth-Century Literature. Essays in Honor of Alan Dugald McKillop*, Chicago University Press for William Marsh Rice University, 1963, pp. 253, 258–63.

80   James Sutherland, 1969

It would be a mistake to set aside the verdict of posterity, or to deny that most of the permanent contributions to literature made during this period were the work of the wits and gentleman writers. To that small class we are indebted for a new kind of English comedy; for a new kind of poetry that came increasingly under the influence of neo-classical standards, but still retained something of the spontaneity of an earlier day; and for the firm establishment of an urbane and unacademic sort of literary criticism suited to the capacity of the intelligent reader. Above all, we are indebted to it for a tradition of easy, polite, familiar discourse that left many delightful traces in the verse of the period, and that created a prose style beautifully poised between the natural and the artificial, enabling the writer to address the reader as an equal, and to express his own thoughts and feelings with accuracy and elegance. Yet outside the world of Dryden and Rochester and Congreve there are many other writers with different claims to our attention. On the fringes of that world, but not really of it, are Clarendon and Burnet, Halifax and Temple, Evelyn and Pepys and Aubrey, poets like Samuel Butler and Charles Cotton, and a political journalist and translator like L'Estrange. Further off, in intellectual worlds of their own, are the great scholar Richard Bentley, churchmen like Robert South or Richard Baxter, lonely republicans like Ludlow and Algernon Sidney, all the men of science, and those, like Sprat and Glanvill, who wrote about it. And still more remote from the vain world of Will's and Locket's, of *MacFlecknoe* and *The Country Wife*, are Bunyan, Fox, Penn, Barclay, and the many other dissenting men and women who lived and thought and wrote with a forthrightness and urgency that expressed one side of this divided and transitional period, and who produced in John Bunyan the greatest imaginative writer of the age.

English Literature of the late Seventeenth Century, Clarendon Press, 1969, p. 31.

RESTORATION HISTORY: THE FUTURE

81   William Haller, 1960

The past historians who have dealt with the Restoration have had principally a political or a biographical interest, leaving quite neglected the social, the economic, the cultural, and, above all, the local history of a great and an extended historical interval. This is a period incredibly rich in diaries, in private correspondence, in family and estate papers, in account books, and in parochial and other local materials. There are, in other words, whole ranges of materials available, and unexploited, which are unhappily very scarce indeed in the earlier half of the century. It is a field, above all, open to younger men and women, who may wish to spend their scholarly lives opening up and elucidating the history of a neglected but an important generation of men.

When this happens, when this period is tackled by a sufficient number of first-rate minds, many questions which have perplexed those of us who work on the other seventeenth-century slope may be clarified or even resolved. We understand, I believe with fair accuracy and sensitivity, the mind of man in the first half of the century; what was the temper and what was the quality of the mind of the Restoration? What happened to Puritanism, which had moulded and given moral texture to men over a full generation and more? What happened to the charitable impulse, so strong in the early seventeenth century, so withered through the whole course of the Restoration? What happened to the gentry, that fabled class which the embattled giants of early seventeenth-century studies have left, as it were, suspended in historical space at precisely 1660? And what happened to the yeomen? To what extent is the ugly political and religious mood of the Restoration rather the reaction of a frightened and a revengeful clique than the mood of a culture, and may not this in turn help to explain the almost comic collapse of Stuart absolutism before the first strong wind of historical reality? One has the conviction that the history of England in this era is to be truly written not from Westminster or Whitehall, but rather from the records of the market towns, from the letters and the accounts of the yeomanry and the gentry, and from the annals of a non-conformity in which for a season was to be seated the moral conscience of England. Historians of this period need to hear the quiet voices, for these were the voices which were in due season to doom a somewhat cheap and ineffectual cult of absolutism, not only because it did violence to the constitutional and historical past, but because its manners were offensive and its morals tawdry. Great themes await those who will undertake the writing of the history of the English Restoration.

The Restoration of the Stuarts, Blessing or Disaster?, Report of a Folger Library Conference, Folger Shakespeare Library, Washington 1960, pp. 50–1.

FURTHER READING

General

The Restoration of the Stuarts, Blessing or Disaster?. Report of a Folger Library Conference, Folger Shakespeare Library, Washington, 1960.

J.P. KENYON, *The Stuarts. A Study in English Kingship*, Ch. IV, Batsford, London, 1958.

The Political Settlement

KEITH FEILING, *A History of the Tory Party, 1640–1714*, Oxford University Press, 1924.

J.P. KENYON, *The Stuart Constitution, 1603–1688: Documents and Commentary*, Cambridge University Press, 1966.

The Religious Settlement

G.R. CRAGG, *From Puritanism to the Age of Reason*, Cambridge University Press, 1950.

NORMAN SYKES, *From Sheldon to Secker. Aspects of English Church History, 1660–1768*, Cambridge University Press, 1959.

The Land Settlement

P.G. HOLIDAY, 'Land sales and repurchases in Yorkshire after the Civil Wars, 1650–1670', *Northern History*, V, 1970, 67–92.

S. MADGE, *The Domesday of Crown Lands*, Routledge, London, 1938.

Economic Policy and Development

J.P. COOPER, 'Economic regulation and the cloth industry in seventeenth-century England', *Transactions of the Royal Historical Society*, XX, 1970.

J.P. COOPER, 'Social and Economic Policies under the Commonwealth', in *The Interregnum: the Quest for a Settlement, 1646–1660*, ed. G.E. Aylmer, Macmillan, 1972.

G.B. HERTZ, *English Public Opinion after the Restoration*, T. Fisher Unwin, London, 1902.

WILLIAM LETWIN, *The Origins of Scientific Economics. English Economic Thought, 1660–1776*, Methuen, London, 1963.

CHARLES WILSON, 'Review article: Economics and politics in the seventeenth century', *Historical Journal*, V, no. 1, 1962, 80–104.

Manners, Morals, and Literature

L.I. BREDVOLD, *The Intellectual Milieu of John Dryden*, Oxford University Press, 1956.

K.M.P. BURTON, *Restoration Literature*, Hutchinson, London, 1958.

INDEX

Act against Tumultuous Petitioning, (1661) 28
Act for Settling Ministers, 53, 56
Act of Confirmation of Judicial Proceedings, 94–5
Act of Indemnity and Oblivion, xxii, 1, 5–8, 91, 94, 103
Act of Settlement, 142, 148
Act of Uniformity, 45, 56–7, 62–3, 65
Agriculture: diversity of, 122; improvement of, 108–9, 113, 133–4, 140, 149, 159
Ailesbury, Lord, xv, 1, 7
Anglicans, 37–40, 51, 53–62, 64–5, 68, 71, 72, 76
Apprenticeship Regulations, 138, 141, 148
Army, 9, 34, 47; pay of, xxiii–xxiv; as purchasers of confiscated land, 88, 96, 104–8

Barrow, Isaac, 176
Barwick, Dr John, 84, 93
Bates, Dr William, 47, 63
Baxter, Richard, xvii, 37, 39, 44, 45, 46, 56, 58, 62–3, 65, 67, 74, 113, 134, 155, 160, 186
Baynes, Capt. Adam, 24, 106
Bishops, 35, 37–8, 40, 41–2, 44–5, 47, 49, 51, 54, 56, 58, 67; lands of, 41, 89, 109; see also Church lands
Britannia Languens, 112, 146
Bosher, Dr Robert S, 38, 40, 50, 70
Boyle, Roger, Earl of Orrey, 194–5
Bramston, Sir John, 9
Breda: Declaration of, xi, xvi, xxii–xxiv, 38, 47, 61, 93; Treaty of, 120
Bridgeman, Orlando, 9
Buckingham, Duke of, 99
Bunyan, John, 73, 186, 198
Burnet, Gilbert, xi, xiii, xxi, 6, 37, 42, 193, 195, 197

Calamy, Edmund, 45, 58, 63

Canterbury, Archbishop of, 81, 96
Capel, Henry, 30
Catholics, 37, 43, 46, 72
Ceremony, 156–8
Charles I, xviii
Charles II: attitude, to Act of Indemnity, 6–8, to government, 183, to land settlement, 37–9, 43–4, 52–4, 65, to social classes, 156–8, to trade, 121; Catholicism of, 60; influence on literature of, 180, 193–7; moral attitude of, 182–3; personality of, xii, xiii, xxi; relation, with Clarendon, 14, with sentry, 30, with Parliament, 17–26, with Privy Council, 15, with town corporations, 34–5; his return without conditions, xi, xiii, xxii, 20, 59
Chesney, Rev. H.E., 82, 92
Cheyney, John, 77
Child, Sir Josiah, 112, 129
Church lands, 81, 83, 85, 88–9, 93–6, 98–9, 109
Clarendon Code, 38, 57, 73, 141
Clarendon, Lord, see Hyde, Edward
Clergy: parish, 39, 45–6, 51–3, 60, 67–9, 89, 191; sermons of, 195–6; taxation of, 65
Coke, Roger, 10, 111–12, 119
Committees: county, 28; of government, 2, 14–15, 144–5, 151; of trade, xxii, 15; see also Commonwealth
Common law, 140, 141
Commonwealth: committees of, xviii–xix; economic policy of, 113–14; failure of, x–xi
Confiscated land, xv–xvi, 81–109; Bill for sales of, 94–6; purchases of, xv, 81, 83–96, 104–7
Consumption, 127–8, 150
Conventicle Act, 38
Convention Parliament, xiv, 6, 9, 25, 27, 94
Convocation, 62, 65, 78

202